LEE'S REAL PLAN
AT GETTYSBURG

The Jedediah Hotchkiss map, used by General Lee during the Gettysburg Campaign. LIBRARY OF CONGRESS

LEE'S REAL PLAN AT GETTYSBURG

Troy D. Harman

STACKPOLE
BOOKS

Published by
STACKPOLE BOOKS
5067 Ritter Road
Mechanicsburg, PA 17055
www.stackpolebooks.com

Maps by Mike Bechthold, mbechtho@wlu.ca

Printed in China

10 9 8 7 6 5 4 3 2 1

FIRST EDITION

Library of Congress Cataloging-in-Publication Data

Harman, Troy D.
    [Cemetery Hill]
    Lee's real plan at Gettysburg / Troy D. Harman.—1st ed.
        p. cm.
    Originally published: Cemetery Hill. 1st ed. Baltimore, MD : Butternut & Blue, 2001.
    Includes bibliographical references and index.
    ISBN 0-8117-0054-2
    1. Gettysburg, Battle of, Gettysburg, Pa., 1863. 2. Lee, Robert E. (Robert Edward), 1807–1870—Military leadership. I. Title.

    E475.53.H34 2003
    973.7'349—dc21
                                                        2003042409

CONTENTS

LIST OF ILLUSTRATIONS

LIST OF MAPS

FOREWORD

So much has been published about the Gettysburg campaign and the battle of Gettysburg over the past 140 years that the reader's first question upon seeing yet another study coming off the printing press could justifiably be "Why?" Why do we need another book about Gettysburg, for surely every facet of the battle and the campaign has by now been studied to death? If the reader's primary interest is in the details of troop movements, battle engagements, and the ebbs and flow of battle, then this study may not be of much interest. But for those whose interests lie in understanding why the battle unfolded as it did, this provocative study is well worth the read.

Much of the challenge of the study of history is centered on the questions of why events unfolded as they did. Conversely, the simplest task for a historian is determining who did what, where, and when, for these building blocks of the historical record are generally readily available. Thus it is with the Gettysburg campaign. Through innumerable documents, including official records and reports, letters, diaries, and reminiscences, historians have pieced together a highly reliable chronology of the Gettysburg campaign, complete with mind-numbing details of regimental movements, unit rosters, and orders of battle.

But when struggling to answer the questions of "why" that surround the battle of Gettysburg, there are fewer elements of certitude. One question that has been examined by historians in the past is: Why did Robert E. Lee conduct the battle as he did? This study provides a fresh and provocative analysis. As the title implies, it is centered on the thesis that the central and unchanged objective of Lee's tactical plans from the late afternoon of July 1 through the failure of Longstreet's assault on July 3 was to "render Cemetery Hill untenable."

In these pages, Troy Harman has assembled an impressive set of arguments to bolster his theory. The historical records of the battle and its participants, presented with the understanding that control of Cemetery Hill meant control of the town of Gettysburg, the surrounding countryside, and the entire road network radiating out of Gettysburg, appear highly supportive of the theory presented here. Equally impressive, Troy has used his detailed knowledge of the battlefield terrain—describing what it looks like today, as well as what it looked like in 1863—to analyze and test his theory. The result is certain to stimulate debate among scholars of the Gettysburg campaign.

This study does not definitively answer all the questions concerning why Robert E. Lee chose to conduct the battle of Gettysburg as he did. Indeed, no study will ever do so; the reasons were known only to those directly involved in the heat of battle—that unique environment of fear, exhilaration, mayhem, and death that we call combat. But it is the task of good historians to posit theories that help explain the known patterns of behavior or chains of events that the historical record has left us. This study does so and is thus good history.

Dr. John A. Latschar
Superintendent, Gettysburg National Military Park
September 2000

ACKNOWLEDGMENTS

Several people deserve special thanks for this work. Foremost is my father, Jim Harman, who passed away on March 16, 2000. He went through a tremendous period of illness during which I wrote most of this book. In the middle of his illness, while on his back with double amputations to his feet and failed kidneys and lungs, he gave this book its first edit. He authored two books in his own right, and I am fortunate that he shared his abilities with me in such a weakened state. He introduced me to a love for history, took me to many historic places while growing up, and always inspired me to dream. He believed that I could do anything, and so I strive to do so. In many ways, I did this in honor of him.

Also supporting and inspiring me has been my wife, Lisa, and my mother, Patricia. Both have stood by me to help me clear many hurdles and have continually given of themselves. I am most indebted to Lisa for her pep talks on the occasions when frustration tried to set in during the creation of this work. Lisa additionally took most of the photographs herein, ran many errands, traveled with me for book presentations, and often listened to my thinking out loud. She encouraged, nurtured, consoled, cheered, and inspired me all the way through. Pursuing this second edition has been invigorated by the birth of our son, Daniel James, on July 20, 2002. He is our inspiration every day. Much thanks and love to my sister and brother-in-law, Michon and Jeff Cale, and Anora and Leland Cale. And likewise to my father- and mother-in-law, Stephen and Carolyne Gohr, who reassured and heartened me several times during this endeavor.

Dr. Paul Gill, a retired professor of history at Shippensburg University, deserves much thanks as an advisor for this work in its master's thesis form. He was the chief advisor on my thesis committee and was meticulous in his proofreading. Dr. Sarah Hughes and Dr. James G. Coolsen were very helpful in this capacity as well. Dr. Paul V. Adams, another professor of history at Shippensburg, instilled in me the courage to undertake the arguments within this book. In a historiography class, Dr. Adams challenged me to write a bold book that is unafraid to offend, rather than an unoffensive one destined to collect dust.

Supervisory Historian Scott Hartwig, at Gettysburg National Military Park (GNMP), and historians Wayne Motts and Al Gambone all read through this book, made editorial remarks, provided feedback, and recommended it. I am grateful for their direction and support. Historians Tom Desjardin, Tim Smith, Garry Adelman, Tony Nicastro, Sue Boardman, and Charlie Fennell have also furnished help in various ways over the last couple years. Thank you for your positive endorsement. Likewise, I am grateful for the backing that Bill and Kathy Pieszak, Mike and Marsha Busichio, Jack Drummond, Chuck Teague, Tony Ten-Barge, Mike Valone, Rich Rollins, and John Winkelman gave throughout the research and writing process.

Much thanks to Ranger Bert Dunkerly, who is stationed at Kings Mountain National Military Park, and Ranger Bill Warder, at Colonial National Historical Park, who continually kept tabs on my progress. Neither would let me procrastinate. Rangers Thomas Holbrook, Rick Bartol, Bert Barnett, Greg Coco, and Matt Atkinson, who are close friends of mine at GNMP, also helped me hammer out some of the issues discussed in the pages that follow. Likewise, ranger and historian Karlton Smith, at GNMP, has freely shared with me excerpts of letters, reports, and other firsthand accounts from his impressive collection of primary sources. Much appreciation also to my good friend Bud Bierbower, who carried out important legwork for me.

Maja Keech, who works in the Prints and Photographs Division of the Library of Congress, aided me greatly. She provided several leads with photographs, furnished contacts, and generally advised on how to proceed with gathering images. Thanks also to Michael Dickerson, with the Photoduplication Service, who promptly processed my image requests from the Library of Congress. Lee Stevens, who oversees the extensive art collection at the State Museum of Pennsylvania in Harrisburg, was most helpful. Sincere thanks to Administrative Assistant Brenda J. Wetzel there, too. Much gratitude to Rebecca Ebert, at Handley Regional Library in Winchester, Virginia, who made it possible to photograph and publish the coveted Hotchkiss Map.

Special thanks to the staff in the Photographic Services Section of Wilson Library at the University of North Carolina for their speedy response. In like manner, I am grateful for the careful attention and time given by Michael Knight, a former specialist with the archives at GNMP, who went the extra mile to supply certain photographs, illustrations, and caption material for this book, and to historian Winona Peterson, who helped process a number of these images. The assistance of GNMP chief curator Mike Vince and his assistant, Paul Sheuchuck, was of great help, too. I am also grateful to historian Kathy Georg Harrison, at GNMP, who has been supportive at each stage and has always been willing to listen and lend insight.

Much gratitude is due to ranger and historian John Heiser, at GNMP, who skillfully designed the maps for the first edition of this work. He has vast experience in the field of cartography and brings an equally impressive store of knowledge of the Civil War to his work. Much appreciation goes out to talented photographer Harry Waters, who captured some difficult close-ups of the Hotchkiss Map, along with Bachelder's Troop Position Map, on film. I also want to thank the devout hobbyists of the battle of Gettysburg who religiously visit and support the park. Many of these visitors first heard my ideas on Cemetery Hill years ago, when they were still obscure, and have stuck with me as I worked them out. They accompanied me on Anniversary Battle Walks, watched my programs on Pennsylvania Cable Network (PCN), or just came along on the early walks when I first tested my theories. This respectful crowd let me work out the theory, supported the concept, and then urged me to press forward with the project until it has now finally appeared in published form.

A warm appreciation also goes out to Jim and Judy McLean, and Christopher Gill of Butternut & Blue, who published the first edition of this book. Their motto of "Quality Books and Quality Service for More than a Decade" is as true behind the scenes as it appears on the surface. Thank you for the professionalism and hard work that were balanced with cordial exchanges.

Finally, to work with Leigh Ann Berry, M. David Detweiler, Tony Hall, and the staff of Stackpole Books is to work with the best. Stackpole's commitment to personal and professional excellence stands out immediately. I am grateful to their people and loyal to their mission.

INTRODUCTION

There is a story of the battle of Gettysburg in 1863 that has not been written. A story that has remained cryptic in form, hidden from history. I am referring to Gen. Robert E. Lee's true tactical plan for Gettysburg: his intention, throughout the battle, to converge his forces upon and to seize Cemetery Hill on the Union center. Lee's training and years of experience as a soldier led him to understand that Cemetery Hill was the key to the Union position, and from the evening of July 1 until the conclusion of the battle on July 3, he held to that belief. When Lee referred in his official report to the general plan at Gettysburg, the objective of that plan was Cemetery Hill.

To understand the thinking behind the theory presented in this book, one needs to forget virtually everything that has previously been accepted as fact about the Confederate strategy at Gettysburg. This is not a book that allows the reader to take away a new idea to apply to his existing view of Lee's battle plan, because the two perspectives are incongruent. Simply stated, the reader cannot hold to the traditional story and understand the concept that is to be explained in the pages that follow. That being said, it must first be understood how the traditional story as it has come down to us has managed for so many years to obscure Lee's true intentions during those fateful July days. To help understand the distinctions between the traditional story and the one about to be put forward, a framework advanced by the history theorist Carl Becker (1877–1945) will prove useful.

1

Becker provided a model that identified two basic types of understanding that develop in our relations to an event in the past:

> The historian cannot deal directly with this event itself, since the event itself has disappeared. What he can deal with directly is a statement about the event. . . . There is thus a distinction of capital importance to be made: the distinction between the ephemeral event which disappears, and the affirmation about the event which persists. For all practical purposes it is this affirmation about the event that constitutes for us the historical fact.[1]

Becker's idea is that the "ephemeral event" is the event as it actually occurred, but that it is fleeting, and true knowledge of it disappears soon after it ends. This is where the "affirmed event," a commonly agreed-upon recollection, takes over.

A practical example of Becker's theory relates to the battlefield: Imagine that there were one hundred men in a company ready to do battle. During the course of their fight, seventy of those men were killed, leaving only thirty survivors. From those thirty, only four made written accounts of the events of the battle. Thus only a small minority of the soldiers who participated in the battle survived to help re-create what actually happened, and still fewer were literate or articulate enough to write down their experiences. Therefore, in Becker's model, in the moments immediately after the battle, as the life's blood of seventy men was shed on the ground, the historian's best opportunity to capture the full story disappeared. The "ephemeral event," which was closer to the actual experience, both chronologically and physically, was lost in the moments immediately following the action.

In the aftermath, left with incomplete information of the event, survivors and enthusiasts begin to piece the story together. Some accounts are more complete than others. Some carry more weight because of the clout of their authors. Some are more descriptive, even more compelling and forceful. Some of the remembrances are tainted with emotions such as fear, pride, or feelings of recrimination toward certain individuals. Some accounts attempt to tell broader stories than the participants were capable of experiencing. Additionally, the victor of the battle wins the war of words as well, while the loser is often unwilling to make a detailed account of his failure. Virtually all of the recollections are corrupted by the soldiers' desire to be remembered in the best possible light. All are in some way flawed. With all of these deficiencies, the accepted story as it emerges hardly represents a foolproof account of the actual event.

As time goes on, the story takes other twists. The participants in the battle come together—through personal written correspondence, by reading each other's published accounts of the event, and in person through gatherings at reunions. During these exchanges, an agreed understanding of the battle is hammered out by a few survivors, each of whom was privy to only certain aspects of it, from his own unit's perspective. With a desperate need to understand the story, a version is agreed upon that smooths over the gaps in knowledge and provides the participants with a longed-for sense of purpose in the event. Once a consensus has been reached, the story becomes indelibly fixed.

The product of this consensus is the "affirmed event," to use Becker's terminology. It is the event as it will be remembered, but not necessarily as it happened. Regrettably, once established, it becomes nearly impossible to dismiss—even if new, seemingly contradictory, evidence is discovered. Consequently, any new version of the story must build around the old consensus and be incorporated into it, even at the expense of logic.

This is precisely what has happened to the understanding of Lee's tactical plan for the battle of Gettysburg. The "ephemeral event" has been lost, and the "affirmed event"—incongruities and all—has survived and is now deeply embedded in the popular consciousness. The object of this work is to attempt to recover the ephemeral event and to arrange Lee's actions more logically within the general plan under which he claimed to have operated.

For a clearer understanding of Lee's tactical plan at Gettysburg, one must first take a closer look at exactly what the battle's "affirmed event" consists of. Starting with the first day, July 1, it is generally agreed that the two armies stumbled into one another at Gettysburg. This accidental meeting grew into a significant action as both armies began to concentrate. The accepted story is that the Army of the Potomac, commanded overall by Union general George G. Meade, won the morning phase of the battle but was outnumbered and outflanked in the afternoon, which led to its retreat through town. South of town, it rallied on heights that Maj. Gen. Oliver O. Howard's XI Corps had occupied in part. Meanwhile, General Lee, for various reasons, missed an opportunity to follow up on his initial success and seize the heights. The first day of the battle then ended, with the Confederates having won but having missed an opportunity to follow up on their success and drive the Federals from the field.

All of this is true enough. The story line is safe, and these broad descriptions of the first day are not really debatable. The problem here is not with the accuracy of this version of the opening day's battle, but rather with the lack of inquiry into the reasons why the fight on July 1 occurred. Historians have been so preoccupied with *how* the battle unfolded that they have neglected to explore the reasons *why* it did so.[2]

Missing from this account, for example, are explanations as to why the Army of the Potomac rallied south on the specific heights they did, and why they fought that day at Gettysburg in the first place. More fundamentally, there is a lack of emphasis on why Lee's Army of Northern Virginia was even in the vicinity of Gettysburg on July 1.[3] Moreover, there is insufficient curiosity as to why Lee's failure to follow up on his first day's success against the Union position was a missed opportunity to win the battle. An inquiry into these questions, or increased thought into their purpose, allows the foundation of Lee's true general plan to be laid.

The *hows* have also prevailed in the study of the fight on July 2. In the accepted version, it is readily agreed that the Union army occupied a J-shaped position, a "fishhook," that stretched over two and a half miles, from Wolf Hill on their right to the vicinity of Little Round Top on their left. As far as Lee's tactics are concerned, the affirmed story does not reveal much depth to the Confederate commander's aims for the second day of battle. The extent of his plans appears to have been the simultaneous attack against the Union flanks, primarily by the corps of Lt. Gen. James Longstreet on the Confederate right and Lt. Gen. Richard S. Ewell on the left. The retelling of the events of July 2 does not reveal Lee's objectives, but is mostly concerned with how each Union corps protected its particular threatened area of the battle line. There are articles, essays, and unit histories of individual actions that attest to this fact. From this traditional perspective, Confederate attacks are seen as disjointed, individual, and unrelated. There appears to have been no deeper purpose behind them because, once again, the accepted version of the story focuses largely on the *how* and not the *why*.

If one were to seriously investigate the *why* questions for July 2, it would become evident that current explanations of Lee's plans are incongruent and incompatible with his overall actions. Why, for example, did

Lee refuse Longstreet's request to march around the Union left flank to get between Meade's army and Washington? And why was Lee seemingly uninterested in Maj. Gen. John Bell Hood's request to swing around and attack Little Round Top indirectly? The fact that Lee rejected both Longstreet's broader strategic move and Hood's more moderate one points to the conclusion that Lee's true tactical aims could not have been focused on merely turning the Union left flank. In light of this, it is illogical to believe that Lee expected Longstreet to swing around Little Round Top and cut off Union access to the Taneytown Road, a favorite concept of the affirmed camp. Furthermore, why did Lee insist to Longstreet that Hood must attack up the Emmitsburg Road (which runs to the west of Little Round Top) on July 2? An answer to this question leads one to consider that Lee did not place the importance upon taking Little Round Top that the accepted history of the battle would have us believe. The commonly held belief that Lee had designated Little Round Top as the key position simply does not add up with Hood's orders for that day.

Ensconced deeply in the affirmed version of the second day of the battle is also the notion that the forward movement of Maj. Gen. Daniel E. Sickles's Union III Corps from Cemetery Ridge toward the Peach Orchard was a sad mistake, if not a direct disobedience of General Meade's orders. In consequence, Sickles has become the villain of the Union army at Gettysburg. His decision to establish an advance defensive line along the Peach Orchard/Emmitsburg Road Ridge has been interpreted by most as a grave error that nearly cost the Union army the battle.[4] One of the major reasons for Sickles's condemnation has been that the affirmed version asserts that he "should have been more concerned about covering Little Round Top, as he was supposed to do, than about occupying the Peach Orchard. That hill was a castle; the orchard was a knight."[5]

The affirmed account of the third day of the battle is even less effective at revealing Lee's real plans. Lee's tactics during this stage of the battle are now so distorted in the public mind that they do not even resemble his own official report to the Confederate War Department. How and why Lee's aims, in the affirmed version, have become so far removed from the true unfolding of events are addressed in the conclusion to this book, as a separate dedicated study is required to deal with this issue in the depth it deserves. Suffice it to say for now that Lee's tactical strategy has been reduced to his order to General Longstreet on July 3 for a single direct assault against the Union center, the attack later known as Pickett's Charge. Regrettably, as far as previous histories are concerned, that was the extent of Lee's plan for the third day of the battle.

If the historian desires a fuller understanding of Lee's tactical aims over the course of July 2 and 3, the accepted sequence of events simply does not provide it. Rather, in encapsulated form, the affirmed version asserts that Lee assaulted the Union flanks on July 2, and after meeting with only limited success, he changed his plan for July 3 to a direct assault against the Union center. In fact, if one wanted to sum up Lee's battle plan for the three days from that perspective, it would go like this: On July 1, the armies met by chance. The two sides sparred and became acquainted, before the Union army retreated through Gettysburg and rallied on some heights south of town. On July 2, Lee ordered a simultaneous attack against both Union flanks in an attempt to turn them. On July 3, having failed to turn the Union flanks, Lee changed his plan to a direct frontal assault against the Union center.

A number of historians maintain that Lee changed his plans for July 3. In *The Gettysburg Campaign: A Study in Command*, Edwin B. Coddington writes, "Now that a well-coordinated attack at an early hour was no longer possible Lee had to scrap his plans for the day and start all over again."[6] George R. Stewart, in *Pickett's Charge: A Micro-history of the Final Attack at Gettysburg*, describes how Lee began to form the idea of Pickett's Charge on the morning of July 3. As Stewart asserts, "This involved a considerable change of plan. First, the point of assault was shifted to the Union right-center. Second, all idea of direct coordination with Ewell's attack was abandoned."[7] Glenn Tucker expresses a similar notion in *High Tide at Gettysburg: The Campaign in Pennsylvania*, noting that Lee's July 2 attacks on Little Round Top and Culp's Hill had "caused the Federal army to concentrate on its flanks; hence, its weakest point must be the center. . . . Lee's attack [for July 3] was simple—to use Pickett's fresh division as the shock troops in an effort to break the Federal center."[8] In a recent essay entitled "Cross Purposes: Longstreet, Lee, and Confederate Attack Plans for July 3 at Gettysburg," William Garrett Piston comes the closest to grasping Lee's general plan but still becomes ensnared in traditional thinking by addressing the question "Why did Lee alter his First Plan?"[9]

It is beyond the scope of this work to fully explore how and why the affirmed version of the battle has so completely diverged from Lee's own official report. In general, however, there is one underlying explanation for this discrepancy. Again, it is that the affirmed camp (with the exception of

Harry Pfanz in most cases, Piston, and perhaps Tucker in *Lee and Longstreet at Gettysburg*) has become preoccupied with understanding the *hows* rather than the *whys* of the battle. If the *whys* were investigated more diligently, then the affirmed explanation of events, I believe, would crumble.

One question, for example, is this: If Lee really did change his plans from a simultaneous flank attack on July 2 to a direct frontal assault on July 3, as the proponents of the affirmed event claim, then why did Lee state in his official report that his "general plan was unchanged" for that day?[10] To believe that Lee changed his plans from one day to the next directly contradicts his own words. Lee also prepared a second report, written in January 1864, nearly six months after the battle, so there was plenty of time for him to reconsider the statement and admit that he changed his plan, if indeed he had. That he did not do so is significant.

Another question worth asking is why, if Longstreet's assault, spearheaded by Pickett's division, was to be a solo operation on July 3, did both Lee and Ewell report, in crystal-clear terms, that elements of Ewell's Second Corps, namely Maj. Gen. Edward Johnson's division supported by Major General Rodes's and Major General Early's divisions, were to assault Culp's Hill at the same time?[11] Moreover, if Lee did not include Culp's Hill in a coordinated attack with Longstreet on July 3, then why did he reinforce General Johnson's position there by nearly 6,000 troops during the early hours of July 3? Was the bolstering of the Culp's Hill assault force really incidental in Lee's plan? In the affirmed version of events, Culp's Hill has become unrelated to Pickett's Charge, and even irrelevant to it.

What has prevented proponents of the consensus view from asking these vital questions? The answer is that the traditional understanding of the battle is falsely shackled to objectives that were never part of Lee's plan. One such misguided objective is the belief that on the second day of the battle, Lee viewed Little Round Top as the key to the Union position. Because the affirmed version continues to mistakenly emphasize this hill, Lee's true goal is destined to remain concealed. As long as Little Round Top remains in such a significant position, General Meade's chief engineer, Maj. Gen. Gouverneur K. Warren, will reign a major hero of the battle with his confirmation of the hill's preeminence; Longstreet or Lee will be blamed for not shifting more forces there; and Hood will appear brilliant in having wanted to swing around behind it. Elsewhere, the Union VI Corps' arrival on the field will go unnoticed behind the heroics of Col. Strong Vincent's brigade atop those rocky heights. At the other end of the Union line, Ewell's attack will appear belated, out of sync, even unrelated to Longstreet's push against the Union left.

Within the accepted version of the third day of the battle, Lee's tactical aim in attacking the Union center is as falsely hitched to the "copse of trees" as his second day's plans are incompatibly linked to Little Round Top. In ordering Longstreet to make this frontal assault, Lee is said to have had his men guide in on several underdeveloped trees, which were barely visible to the Confederate attackers who were deployed in the deep swales just east of Seminary Ridge.

Several questions arise when the historian dares to ask why Lee should have wanted to place the focus on those trees. For instance, what advantage did a breakthrough at that point of the Union line offer over penetration through some other part of the line? Was the angle in the stone wall there really a salient of military significance, or was it merely a jut in the wall? Where were the Confederate attackers to go once they had broken through that point? Would the victor of Second Manassas, Fredericksburg, and Chancellorsville really commit over 10,000 men to an attack designed to stop at a ridge that had no real inherent tactical value? And, once again, how could Lee have changed his plans from attacking the Union flanks on the second day of the battle to charging the center on the third if, as he recorded in his official report, "the general plan was unchanged" from July 2 to July 3?

The answers to these questions, as well as many others regarding Lee's real tactical plan at Gettysburg, cannot be satisfactorily answered within the traditional story of the battle. As long as the agreed version is anchored in the minds of historians, the answers will remain hidden.

So, what was Lee's real plan at Gettysburg? To discover that, one must be bold. Where there are gaps in understanding his tactics, one must bridge them with feasible hypotheses. The missing pieces must be included to help assemble the whole puzzle rather than leaving them out because they do not seem to fit. In reconstructing Lee's true tactical plan at Gettysburg, one must make assumptions about how the pieces fit together completely and logically, and break with the affirmed version where it obstructs reason.

CHAPTER 1

Why Lee Targeted
Cemetery Hill

Gen. Robert E. Lee focused his attention on Cemetery Hill for three main reasons. These had to do with his army's failure to win the battle the first day, the importance of the road junctions the hill dominated, and the inherent weakness of the Federals' battle line as it had developed by July 2.

The first of Lee's reasons concerned his army's freedom of manuever after the events around Gettysburg on July 1, the outcome of which threatened to rob him of the initiative in the campaign that had begun on June 16 when he had ordered the Army of Northern Virginia across the Maryland border.

By the afternoon of July 1, Lt. Gen. A. P. Hill's Confederate Third Corps was pressing an attack west of Gettysburg over Willoughby Run and toward McPherson's Woods, while Lt. Gen. Richard S. Ewell's Second Corps made its advance south and eventually through Gettysburg itself, toward the high ground that dominated to the south and southeast—features known as Cemetery Hill, East Cemetery Hill, and Culp's Hill. Ewell, however, was held below these heights by both the remnants of Maj. Gen. Oliver O. Howard's Union XI Corps and Maj. Gen. John F. Reynolds's I Corps.

Ewell's shortcoming here would have serious repercussions for Lee, because Gettysburg and its surrounding area was the meeting point for roads spreading out into all parts of southern Pennsylvania—a fact of which the

Army of the Potomac was also well aware. Staff Officer Frank Haskell, of Brig. Gen. John Gibbon's II Corps headquarters, concurred: "Gettysburg was a point of strategic importance—a great many roads, some ten or twelve at least, concentrated there, so the army could easily converge to, or, should a further march be necessary, diverge from, this point."[1]

Lee, too, would have seen the network of roads emanating from Gettysburg on his map, and, as would any good West Pointer, he would have known that it would be advantageous to locate his army at the nexus of those roads and secure all points of entry and exit. Control of the roads would then have provided his army with the largest number of options for manuever, a vitally important consideration for any invading force. Maintaining this freedom of action followed one of the Napoleonic maxims that Lee and his fellow West Point cadets would have been taught, that "an invading army should maneuver to force an enemy to assail it in a chosen position."[2] In other words, in enemy territory, fighting defensively on ground of one's own choosing was the preferred option, and going on the offensive was to remain only as an alternative. If a general did choose offensive over defensive operations, to ensure victory he would be committed to follow through completely after any successful engagement in order, as Napoleon warned, to "prevent the beaten enemy from rallying."[3]

When Lee elected to continue the battle during the afternoon of July 1 on the fields west and north of Gettysburg, he had cast his lot with offense, thereby abandoning the more advantageous choice to fight defensively in enemy territory, perhaps by a move originally toward the Pennsylvania state capital of Harrisburg, some forty miles to the north. The absence of Maj. Gen. J. E. B. Stuart and his Confederate cavalry, however, greatly diminished the prospects of moving the greater army farther north. So, as Lee sanctioned a continuance of the battle on July 1, he allowed the Union forces to dictate the choice of battleground and began to surrender the strategic initiative. His options were narrowing by the minute.

The situation was not helped by the disposition of his own troops. As Ewell halted his advance shy of Cemetery Hill on the afternoon of July 1 and asked Lee whether he should continue his advance on the Union positions, Lee realized, to his chagrin, that he was unable to provide Ewell with any support. The only available forces were to the west, and of these, Lt. Gen. James Longstreet's First Corps was partially blocked by Confederate supply wagons along the Chambersburg Pike, and A. P. Hill's Third Corps was already committed, with two of its three divisions having been

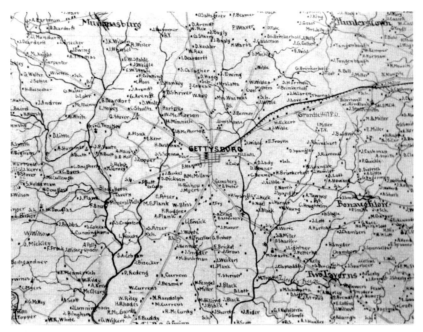

A magnified view of the strategically significant road network through Gettysburg as shown on the Hotchkiss map. LIBRARY OF CONGRESS

mangled by Reynolds's Union I Corps above Willoughby Run. Neither would be able to provide reinforcements to Ewell.

By the close of the battle's first day, Lee was in no-man's-land, tactically speaking. His optimum objective would have been to manuever his army toward a defensive battle. But this course had been forfeited; Lee had begun to surrender the initiative and had given up the optimum by choosing to fight offensively. Although by the end of the day he had gained control of Seminary Ridge and Benner's Hill and pushed the Federals out of the town, he had failed to close out the victory by gaining control of Cemetery Hill. It was therefore imperative to resume the offensive as quickly as possible early on the morning of July 2 and drive the Federals from the field completely before the Union army concentrated. Therefore, in simple terms, the first reason that Lee desired to take Cemetery Hill, throughout the remainder of the battle, was to finish what was started on July 1.

The second reason Lee desired to seize Cemetery Hill is a natural offshoot of the first. Cemetery Hill was inadvertently the best ground for Lee's troops from the moment he made the decision to concentrate the Army of Northern Virginia at Gettysburg. In 1864, Brig. Gen. Henry J. Hunt, who had commanded the Union artillery during the battle, testified to a sub-committee of the 38th Congress: "[Gettysburg] is a natural place, I should think . . . so many roads meeting there. If [Lee] wanted to concentrate, it would be the most natural place for him to do so."[4]

If the Union army's left wing, under General Reynolds, had not been as far north as it was on July 1, then perhaps Lee would have moved gradually and leisurely toward Gettysburg, without alarm or harassment, and gained control of the roads there. If this had been his intention, then Cemetery Hill would, at some point, have become his destination, because it commanded that nerve center of roads. A French historian of the Civil War, Louise Phillipe, Comte de Paris, drove this point home when he recorded, "Cemetery Hill completed, in a tactical point of view, the strategic advantages presented by Gettysburg: it commanded the town and all the roads adjoining it."[5] Therefore, by virtue of being at the heart of the crossroads, Cemetery Hill was perhaps the most advantageous ground from the beginning.

Even if Lee had not intended to deliberately gain the key road center around Cemetery Hill, taking that strategic spot must have entered his thinking during the afternoon of July 1, as the fight west and north of town was developing. His adversaries certainly wasted no time in spotting its value. Maj. Gen. Carl Schurz of the Union XI Corps thought back to the early afternoon of that day when he recalled, "If the enemy was bringing on the whole or a large part of his army . . . then we had to look for a strong position in which to establish and maintain ourselves until reinforced or ordered back. Such a position was easily found at the first glance. It was on Cemetery Hill, which was to play so important a part in the battle to follow."[6]

If Lee was not as keen and quick as Schurz in noticing the commanding nature of Cemetery Hill, then, at the very latest, he must have considered its importance around 4 P.M. during the Federal retreat through the town. After the war, Maj. St. Clair A. Mulholland, who had commanded the 116th Pennsylvania Infantry, of the Union II Corps, expressed what would have been obvious to the retreating Union survivors and to everyone on the field, including Lee. Mulholland confidently recounted of that afternoon: "Our defeat seemed to be complete. Our troops were flowing through the streets of the town in great disorder, closely pursued by the Confederates, the retreat fast becoming a rout and in a very few minutes the enemy would have been in possession of Cemetery Hill, the key to the position, and the battle of Gettysburg would have gone into history as a Confederate victory."[7]

Certainly, Maj. Gen. Winfield Scott Hancock, commander of the Union II Corps, who helped rally and organize the survivors on Cemetery Hill, wasted no time in recognizing the location's strategic importance. When he inspected Union positions to determine for army commander General Meade whether the rest of the Army of the Potomac should be transferred from the Pipe Creek Line in Maryland north to Gettysburg, he undoubtedly saw that the valuable network of roads that the army would have to traverse from Maryland dovetailed at Gettysburg—and that their point of intersection was Cemetery Hill. Hancock reported: "Orders were at once given to establish a line of battle on Cemetery Hill. . . . The position just on the southern edge of Gettysburg, overlooking the town and commanding the Emmitsburg and Taneytown roads and the Baltimore turnpike."[8] This is probably the reason why he agreed with XI Corps commander Maj. Gen. Oliver O. Howard to rally the troops there. Hancock remembered: "As it was necessary at once to establish order in the confused mass of his [Howard's] troops on Cemetery Hill and the Baltimore pike, I lost no time in conversation, but at once rode away and bent myself to the pressing task of making such dispositions as would prevent the enemy from seizing that vital point."[9] In correspondence five and a half years after the battle, Hancock also said that General Meade was able to get a full view of the battlefield by "riding up the crest of Cemetery Hill."[10]

Even a lowly lieutenant in Company I, 8th Louisiana Infantry, realized that "the enemy was posted on Cemetery Hill about 600 yards from town & had command of every place near town or around it."[11] It was obvious to many that day that "Cemetery Hill . . . perfectly commanded the town, and the entire country over which the Confederates must pass to attack . . . [as a] central tower of strength."[12]

General Howard must have learned of the importance of that hill before noon on July 1, shortly before his XI Corps began arriving on the field. As units arrived, he ordered them out to the north of town to extend the Union I Corps line, whose defensive position stretched along the fields west of Gettysburg. Meanwhile, he left Brig. Gen. Adolph von Steinwehr's division in reserve on Cemetery Hill, which was the obvious point to fall back to if necessary. Howard left no doubts about the importance of Cemetery Hill when he noted that "the highest point at the cemetery commanded every eminence within easy range."[13]

Howard was not the first to make such plans. Around 10 A.M., if not earlier, General Reynolds began to organize a defense in depth, committing all three of his divisions, which would resist Confederate entry west of the town. Their position was centered behind Willoughby Run on McPherson's Ridge about two miles in front of Cemetery Hill. Had Reynolds not been shot and killed by a Rebel sharpshooter that morning, the Cemetery Hill position likely still would have been occupied by Union troops by day's end. Military historian A. T. Cowell asserted, "It has been claimed that Reynolds would have retired to Cemetery Hill had he not been killed. . . . Captain [Joseph G.] Rosengarten [of Reynolds's staff] has even asserted that Reynolds had designated Cemetery Hill as the point which Howard was to occupy."[14]

Plainly stated, the purpose of Union resistance west and north of Gettysburg during the morning of July 1 was for the first Federal troops on the scene to create a cushion of space and time between the location of the opening clashes and the coveted ground of Cemetery Hill. Reynolds, one of the first senior Union officers to arrive, calculated that by the time his advance troops had contested every foot of this ground, other elements of the army's left wing would have arrived, thus assuring that Cemetery Hill would remain in Federal hands.

Even if Reynolds did not live to see the full ramifications of his actions, General Howard certainly came to understand that preserving Cemetery Hill was imperative to conducting a prolonged battle around Gettysburg. Having lost the town to the Confederates, without control of the hill the rest of the Army of the Potomac had no point at which to converge. Again, many of the other Union corps, marching north from Mary-

---

OPPOSITE PAGE: Following the fighting west and north of town in the morning and early afternoon of July 1, the Union army fell back through the town and set up artillery and infantry on Cemetery Hill. The hill's gradual slope allowed the Union the advantage of massing their guns side by side and firing outward in all directions. But the geography of this position, with three roads—Baltimore Pike, the Taneytown Road, and Emmitsburg Road—converging in a "V," or the bend of a fishhook, made it a glaringly obvious salient position. Protruding forward, it soon drew relentless crossfire from both Confederate sharpshooters in and around town and Confederate artillery from surrounding positions.

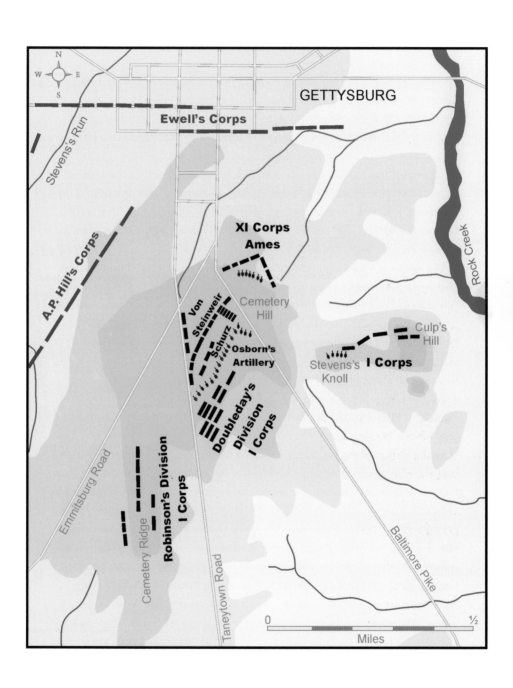

GETTYSBURG

Ewell's Corps

A.P. Hill's Corps

Stevens's Run

XI Corps
Ames

Von
Steinweir

Schurz

Cemetery
Hill

Osborn's
Artillery

Culp's
Hill

Stevens's
Knoll

I Corps

Doubleday's
Division
I Corps

Robinson's Division
I Corps

Emmitsburg Road

Cemetery Ridge

Taneytown Road

Baltimore Pike

Rock Creek

N
W   E
S

0   ½
Miles

land, had to travel the Emmitsburg Road, Taneytown Road, and Baltimore Pike to join the battle, and these roads all came together at Cemetery Hill. Even the Hanover Road, which ran east-west and which the Union V Corps traveled, was very accessible to this all-important piece of high ground. Reynolds knew Cemetery Hill was the point of nexus; Howard rediscovered that truth; and Hancock finally confirmed that fact when he arrived with the II Corps and chose to rally the I and XI Corps there.

The third and perhaps most important reason why Cemetery Hill appealed to Lee as the key to victory lay in its spearhead position along the curvature of the Union line. It is well documented that the high ground occupied by the Federal forces by the late evening of July 1 assumed the shape of a fishhook, stretching from Wolf Hill and Culp's Hill on the right, around Cemetery Hill and along Cemetery Ridge, to the north slope of Little Round Top on the far left. Lt. Frank Haskell of General Gibbon's II Corps divisional staff accurately discerned that "the [Federal] line of battle as it was established, on the evening of the 1st, and morning of the 2nd of July was in the form of the letter, 'U,' the troops facing outwards, and the 'Cemetery,' which is at the point of the sharpest curvature of the line, being due South of the town of Gettysburg."[15] Cemetery Hill became a salient where the Union line protruded toward the Confederate position, the most vulnerable sector of their defensive posture.

The affirmed version of the battle of Gettysburg obscures this third reason by emphasizing that the fishhook gave the Union forces the advantage of interior lines, allowing the speedy movement of troops and materiel, as well as fast and secure communications. This, of course, is true, however there is another, equally relevant detail that has been lost but that is crucial to understanding the true nature of the battle. The shape of the Union line made it, in one way, more dangerous than advantageous. The position at the cemetery made it a natural enemy target—a salient open to attack on three sides if the Confederates could converge a significant number of men on it. Its vulnerability lay in the basic military principle that a salient formed by a protusion or angle in a defensive line is susceptible to crossfire. Defenders, at any given point on the defensive angle, are also at half strength. The troops all fire out, which prevents either side of the angle from supporting the other. There is no converging fire on an enemy, but rather dispersed fire. This would have been apparent to any West Pointer at the time, especially an experienced tactician such as Robert E. Lee.

So Cemetery Hill was not only an exposed position in the Union line, but also the most defensively susceptible position to converging fire. Over the next two days, Confederate sharpshooters in town and Southern artillerists surrounding the arc crisscrossed Cemetery Hill relentlessly in an effort to produce this effect. Therefore, Cemetery Hill, as the bastion of the Union salient, along with Culp's Hill and the northernmost region of Cemetery Ridge, surfaced as the immediate keys to a Confederate victory. The vulnerable outlay of the Union line there did not go unnoticed by Col. Edward Porter Alexander, who, during the early part of the battle, commanded an artillery battalion in Longstreet's First Corps. Alexander dogmatically claimed that "this salient upon Cemetery Hill offered the only hopeful point of attack upon the enemy's entire line, as will more fully appear in the accounts of the different efforts made at various places during the battle."[16]

Lee, without question, would have realized this same truth immediately after the Union position began to take shape on the evening of July 1, and his actions throughout the course of the battle revealed this. The Confederate tactical plan on July 2, then, had to involve converging Southern forces at that salient. With this accomplished, Lee would cripple, if not destroy, part of Meade's army, while placing the Army of Northern Virginia at the nerve center from which all key roads branched out from Gettysburg. The salient at Cemetery Hill, then, had to be the focus of action as the second day of battle began.

CHAPTER 2

The Hours before
the Second Day

During the early hours of July 2, a day that would prove momentous to both armies at Gettysburg, Dr. J. S. Dorsey Cullen, a surgeon attached to the Confederate First Corps, found Lee and Longstreet together on Seminary Ridge, gazing east across open farmlands toward Cemetery Hill, apparently deep in discussion. Cullen later recalled the meeting to General Longstreet: "About three o'clock in the morning, while the stars were shining, you left your headquarters and rode to General Lee's, where I found you sitting with him after sunrise looking at the enemy on Cemetery Hill. I rode then into Gettysburg, and was gone some two hours, and when I returned found you still with General Lee."[1]

From Dr. Cullen's recollections, we can imagine Lee and Longstreet looking out at the Union campfires extending out from Cemetery Hill along Cemetery Ridge, and for several hours contemplating their next move. It is very likely that during their discussions, Lee expressed his opinion about focusing his army's attack for July 2 against Cemetery Hill, which, after all, had been the focal point of the enemy's defensive line at the close of the first day's battle.

This assumption would concur with what is known about their discussions from around 5:00 the previous evening, when Longstreet recorded that he found Lee on the vantage point of Seminary Ridge, watching the enemy concentrate on Cemetery Hill. As Longstreet remarked, "He pointed out their position to me."[2]

Augustus Kollner painted this view entitled, "Gettysburg Pennsylvania From Seminary Hill, 1864," just a year after the battle. The artist's perspective was from the juncture of Seminary Avenue and Fairfield Road, the same view General Lee had of the key position through much of the battle. Looming in the background are the heights of Cemetery Hill crowned with the woods of Ziegler's Grove on the left, and the woods on the southern edge of the Evergreen Cemetery to the right. This view demonstrates how Cemetery Hill controlled the town at the time of the battle. GETTYSBURG NATIONAL MILITARY PARK ARCHIVES

After surveying Cemetery Hill through his field glasses, Longstreet suggested his grand plan of shifting the focus of the battle to the south and marching around the left flank of the Union army. In doing so, he hoped to cut the Emmitsburg and Taneytown Roads and place the Army of Northern Virginia between General Meade and Washington, D.C., thus forcing the Federals onto the offensive with an attack over more easily defended ground of the Confederates' own choosing. But Lee disagreed, retorting forthrightly, "No, the enemy is there, and I am going to attack him there."[3] At 5 P.M. on July 1, "the enemy is there" could refer only to the Union salient hastily established that afternoon on Cemetery Hill. Little Round Top was barely involved in the battle at that point.

Longstreet clearly understood Lee's intentions, because he later recalled: "I saw he was in no frame of mind to listen to further argument at that time, so I did not push the matter.[4] Lee's attitude did not ultimately dissuade Longstreet, however, and he noted his own determination "to renew the subject the next morning."[5] Longstreet had likely reopened the discussion when Dr. Cullen saw them both in the predawn hours of July 2.

There is more evidence that Lee's early-morning conversation with Longstreet centered on plans to take Cemetery Hill. During the evening of July 1, Lee held a meeting with General Ewell, commander of the Second Corps, and two of his division commanders, Generals Early and Rodes, on the back porch of a small house north of town, near the road to Carlisle.[6] During their conference, Lee explored the possibility of the Second Corps undertaking a direct offensive against Cemetery Hill the following morning. General Early responded first and advised against a frontal assault on "Cemetery Hill and the rugged hills on the left of it [Culp's Hill and Wolf Hill, as seen from Confederate lines]," because "it would inevitably be [taken only] at very great loss."[7] Instead, he contended, the attack could be better made from the Confederate right, primarily because of "the more practicable nature of the ascents on that side of the town."[8] James Power Smith, of Ewell's staff, reiterated the same thought, commenting that the ascent of the Union position, from the Confederate right, offered a "more gradual slope affording opportunity for success against the Cemetery Hill."[9]

It is obvious from this meeting between Lee and Ewell's Second Corps generals that Cemetery Hill remained the focus of their discussion. Only the direction from which it would be assailed was called into question. As further evidence of this, Lee even asked Ewell, Early, and Rodes, "interrogatively," "Then perhaps I had better draw you around towards my right, as the line will be very long and thin if you remain here [to the north], and the enemy may come down and break through it?"[10]

The Comte de Paris stated it this way: "He [Lee] even thought for a moment of abandoning [the town of] Gettysburg, in order to bring back the Second Corps to his right and concentrate all his forces in that direction."[11] In retrospect, the comte believed, "it would have been the wisest and most skillful course to pursue. He discarded this idea upon the assurances given by Ewell that his troops could attack and carry Cemetery Hill as soon as Longstreet had broken the lines of the Federal left."[12] It should be added here that from that point on, the goal for all three divisions in Ewell's Corps—the third division to arrive being commanded by Maj. Gen. Edward Johnson—was the capture of Cemetery Hill. Lee did not agree to leave Ewell there for any other purpose. Even General Johnson's division, which was ordered to assault Culp's Hill over the next two days would do so because Lee believed it commanded Cemetery Hill. As Gen. Jubal Early explained, "It was determined with [Johnson's] division to get possession of a wooded hill to the left of Cemetery Hill, which it commanded."[13] Ewell repeated the same thought in 1878, asserting, "But Culp's Hill occupied rendered Cemetery Hill untenable."[14]

It is clear that Lee was investigating every means available to take the enemy's position on Cemetery Hill. He was not exploring any other option, such as the seizure of Little Round Top, not during the evening conference with Ewell on July 1 or at any other time. Instead, Cemetery Hill remained the central goal for Lee, because he "attached great importance to the capture of this height, which seemed to him to be the key to all the enemy's positions." [15]

It is also evident that the idea for Longstreet's July 2 attack on the Union left flank was first raised during that conference with Ewell and his senior officers. Why was Longstreet to attack the Union left on July 2? Because Lee became persuaded, on the evening of July 1 by Ewell, Early, and Rodes, that Cemetery Hill was more easily assailable from the Confederate right. It is only natural to assume that Lee carried this information to Longstreet in the early hours of July 2. If Longstreet "renewed the subject" that morning of an alternative plan to an attack on Cemetery Hill, then it is feasible that assailing Cemetery Hill from the Confederate right was at the heart of their conversation when Dr. Cullen spotted them. It must have been a lively discussion.

Because Longstreet's attack against the Union left began only three hours before sundown on July 2, it is safe to assume that he did not immediately endorse the suggestions of Ewell and his Second Corps generals. More likely, there was a serious debate between Longstreet and Lee during the early hours of July 2, which produced a need for the Union left to be scouted. And this is where Capt. Samuel R. Johnston, a topographical engineer on Lee's staff, entered the picture.

It is well known that Lee sent Johnston out around 4 A.M. to investigate the Union left, and that he reached the vicinity of the famous Peach Orchard down to Houck's Ridge between 4 A.M. and 6 A.M. There is some question, however, as to exactly how far he traveled. Perhaps he got as far as Big Round Top, but maybe not as far as Little Round Top, which is often presumed. In a postwar correspondence with former Confederate general Lafayette McLaws, dated June 27, 1892, Johnston claimed that, "following along that ridge in the direction of the round top across the Emmitsburg road [I] got up on the slopes of round top, where I had a commanding view."[16] This assertion, made twenty-nine years after the battle, is suspect. If

Johnston indeed climbed to the vantage point he professed in his letter to have reached (a view that could only have been gained from Little Round Top), he would have seen Brig. Gen. John Buford's two brigades of Union cavalry down below prior to their reassignment away from the field. Moreover, he would have discovered General Sickles's Union III Corps of nearly 9,500 infantrymen, whose flank was being protected by Buford's cavalry.

That Johnston did not see them is not a profound mystery, but rather a revelation that he did not get as far as he claimed. What is more likely is that he reached Big Round Top, which was heavily wooded and would have concealed the substantial number of Federal cavalry and infantry arrayed to the north. This theory is substantiated by Captain Johnston's own account, which states that he "rode along the base of round top to beyond the ground that was occupied by General Hood, and where there was later on a cavalry fight."[17] Johnston was presumably referring to the Union cavalry charge made by Brig. Gen. Elon Farnsworth against Hood's forces at Big Round Top on July 3. Another possibility is that Johnston reached Bushman Hill, considered at that time part of the Round Tops by the local residents. Bushman Hill served as the launching point for Farnsworth's Charge.[18]

Whether Johnston made it to either of the Round Tops is unclear. What is clear, however, is that Lee was surprised that his scout covered as much ground as he did. Indeed, Lee had not expected Captain Johnston to go that far, suggesting that the Round Tops were not among those areas Lee intended for reconnaissance. When he returned to Lee's headquarters around 7 A.M., Johnston recalled in his letter to McLaws: "[Lee] looked up, saw me and at once called me to him, and on the map that he was holding I sketched the route over which I had reconnoitered. He was surprised at my getting so far, but showed plainly that I had given him valuable information."[19] Writing earlier, in 1878, Johnston recounted: "I stood behind General Lee and traced on the map the route over which I had made the reconnaissance. When I got to the extreme right . . . on Little Round Top, General Lee turned and looking at me, said, "Did you get there[?]"[20]

Lee's curious puzzlement over the breadth of Johnston's reconnaissance is one of the early clues that Little Round Top was not a major part of Lee's tactical plan for July 2. Regarding the news that Johnston brought him, Lee told General Longstreet, "I think you had better move on," his diplomatic way of ending the discussion.[21]

CHAPTER 3

The Importance of Little Round Top

To believers of the affirmed event, the suggestion that the capture of the Round Tops on the Union left were not part of Lee's original tactical plan is tantamount to blasphemy. The accepted interpretation contends that Little Round Top was the obvious key to the entire Union position. A later chapter will explain how it came to be viewed this way. However, on the evening of July 1, and even during the early afternoon of July 2, a Confederate attack against Little Round Top was not considered by Lee as imperative to victory. General Longstreet himself commented on this misconception of Lee's plans:

> The importance of [Little] Round Top, as a *point d'appui* [meaning a point of support, or the key strategic point of a battle line] was not appreciated until after the attack. General Meade seems to have alluded to it as a point to be occupied, "if practicable," but in slighting manner as to show that he did not deem it of great importance [and only later when some senior officer] threw a force into Round Top that [it] transformed, as if by magic, into a Gibraltar.[1]

Longstreet's words provide strong evidence against the significance of Little Round Top to Lee's plans. His message was clear: Little Round Top was not the focus for the right wing of Lee's army. Statistics back up this supposition: 1,819 Confederates assaulted Little Round Top on July 2 as a last-minute shift, and reinforcements never followed. In contrast, Culp's Hill on the opposite flank was attacked over a two-day period, with 10,000 men. If Little Round Top had been vital to Confederate strategy, the attack there would have been reinforced from the beginning.[2]

What, then, were General Lee's real objectives for his right wing? Brig. Gen. Henry J. Hunt, Meade's chief of artillery, explained the plans most observantly in his postwar account of the action on the second day:

> It would appear . . . that General Lee mistook the few troops on the Peach Orchard ridge in the morning for our main line, and that by taking and sweeping up the Emmitsburg road under cover of his batteries, he expected to "roll up" our lines to Cemetery Hill. That would be an "oblique order of battle," in which the attacking line, formed obliquely to its opponent, marches directly forward, constantly breaking in the end of his enemy's line and gaining his rear. General Longstreet was ordered to form the divisions of Hood and McLaws on Anderson's right [Maj. Gen. Richard H. Anderson commanded the right flank division of A. P. Hill's III Corps], so as to envelop our left and drive it in.[3]

To find out what the Confederate tactics did and did not entail, let us consider the meaning of Hunt's analysis of Lee's battle plan, while at the same time adding other facts to support Hunt's observations. To begin with, notice that Hunt's assessment did not portray Little Round Top as a Confederate objective. For that matter, he did not even place Longstreet's advance on a track toward Little Round Top. Instead, Hunt lined up Maj. Gen. John Bell Hood's division of Longstreet's corps to follow a different route, which Hood himself spelled out plainly in a letter to Longstreet after the war. In that letter, Hood recorded that General Longstreet had stated three times on July 2 that his orders were to attack "up the Emmitsburg Road."[4] The Emmitsburg Road does not lead to Little Round Top.

Continuing this thought, Hunt was correct to interpret, in the strictest literal terms, that the attack was to guide in on the Emmitsburg Road. He did so because he fully comprehended where that route led. Advocates of the affirmed event cannot understand Hood's orders, because these orders contradict the importance that has since been attached to Little Round Top. Their interpretation of events has Hood attacking at right angles to the Taneytown Road, immediately east of Little Round Top, which is entirely incongruent with the orders he received from Longstreet on more than one occasion. If the affirmed version gives any thought to Hood's orders in terms of the assault's direction, its holders interpret "Emmitsburg Road" very loosely; they chalk up the usage of these words to mere semantics, or they fall back on the belief that no battle plan survives first impact freeing them to pursue countless courses and objectives. Hunt pursued the literal interpretation of Hood's orders because he fully grasped Lee's real plan, which led the Confederate commander northeast toward Cemetery Hill rather than away from it.

Hunt offers another fine insight: He states that Lee ordered an oblique order of attack for his right wing, in which the advancing force would strike the enemy at a forty-five-degree angle. Lee favored this maneuver, having used it the previous year at Seven Pines, Gaines's Mill, Fraizer's Farm, and Malvern Hill.[5] It was a favored tactic among other Civil War generals as well, its popularity tied to its mention in Baron Antoine Henri de Jomini's influential *Treatise on Grand Military Operations*, written during Napoleon's military ascendancy and first published in 1804.[6]

Perfected by Frederick the Great of Prussia during the 1750s and employed by Napoleon a few decades later, this tactical maneuver in theory offered the attacker the advantage of striking his enemy on the diagonal, yet with full impact, while the enemy was out of position and could not fire back. The defender then had to reorganize and extend his flanked line or change direction while under a deadly fire. The angular direction of the attack caused several other problems for the defender. First, by design, the forty-five-degree approach permitted the entire front of the attacking force to fire, whereas only the flanked end of the defender's line could return a volley. Second, the sudden forty-five-degree left (in this instance) swing would stagger the attacker's line, baiting the defender's attention to the right while the rapidly building parts flanked his left. The lead brigades of Maj. Gen. Lafayette McLaws's division, for example, attempted to do just that,

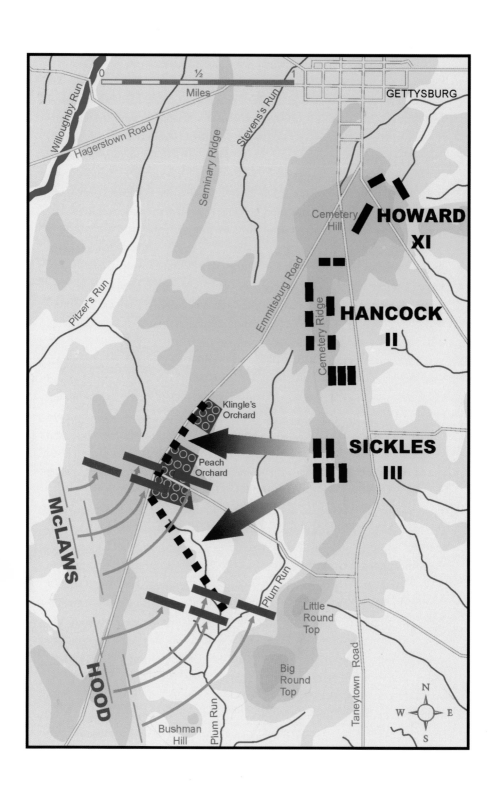

albeit somewhat disjointedly, against the Peach Orchard position on July 2. A third problem the oblique caused the defender had to do with the angle at which the attacker's bullets were being fired. The angle allowed more of them to find their mark, which is very similar to the principle of an enfilade or even converging fire. When viewed this way, an oblique attack offered the attacker an even greater chance for impact than with a direct assault.

The drawback to an oblique attack was that for it to succeed, it required the defender to react slowly or not at all. For the attacker to increase his chance of success, he needed to strike quickly and vigorously. If the maneuver was carried off properly, then the defender's flank would be surrounded and rolled up diagonally.

An assessment of the ground on the Union left, where this oblique attack was ordered on July 2, clearly shows that it was geographically suited for just such a tactic. First of all, the Peach Orchard along the Emmitsburg Road ridge was a commanding location for supporting artillery, far superior, in this respect, to the southernmost portion of Cemetery Ridge directly opposite it. This part of the ridge was "gradually diminishing in elevation," making it a poor artillery position.[7] Essentially, it is a very low bottom from which artillery pieces would have difficulty firing on the Peach Orchard, a mere 800 yards due west. This is because the gradual rise of terrain toward the Emmitsburg Road would make it difficult for Union gunners to raise their cannons' muzzles high enough to project that far.

From a Confederate perspective, it would have been obvious that guns posted in the orchard could bombard their opponents below with every available shell. To the left of this low portion of Cemetery Ridge stood

---

OPPOSITE PAGE: Contrary to popular belief, Lee's general plan did not include an attack on Little Round Top, but rather adhering strictly to an attack "up the Emmitsburg Road." Lee did not intend for the extreme right flank of his army to become bogged down with climbing up and down Big Round Top before attacking up the rocky heights of Little Round Top. As he clearly stated in his official report, troops on these heights "embarrassed [and] delayed" Longstreet's movements on July 2 and July 3. After the war, Longstreet wrote that Little Round Top was not the "point of support," but rather an unexpected obstacle in the plan of driving the Union line in north toward Cemetery Hill and the town of Gettysburg.

The western face of Little Round Top looking from the "Slaughter Pen," or lower Devil's Den. With its many crags and boulders, it was a treacherous position to attack, which may account for Lee's wishes to skirt past it when driving the Union line toward Cemetery Hill and the town. PHOTOGRAPH BY LISA HARMAN

Little Round Top, which provided height to the far left of that position, but it was so steep and rugged as to render it inaccessible to more than a few pieces of artillery. Capt. Frank C. Gibbs, commanding Battery L, 1st Ohio Light Artillery, Union V Corps, attested, "The rocky nature of the ground compelled us to unhitch our horses and place our guns in position by hand."[8]

From the point of view of the Confederate artillery, Little Round Top presented merely an inconvenience to the placement of their batteries in the Peach Orchard. In fact, the orchard also offered a more advantageous artillery position to the Union III Corps under Maj. Gen. Daniel E. Sickles than that portion of the line it originally was to occupy. To this effect, General Hunt, chief of Union artillery, declared: "Although much longer, [the Peach Orchard] afforded excellent positions for our artillery; its occupation would cramp the movements of the enemy, bring us nearer his lines, and afford us facilities for taking the offensive. It was, in my judgment, the better line of the two, provided it were strongly occupied."[9]

The most significant artillery advantage that the orchard position afforded the Confederates on July 2, however, was that guns there could fire obliquely, toward the northern portion of Cemetery Ridge and Cemetery Hill. The Emmitsburg Road ridge, on which the Peach Orchard stood, forms a nearly forty-five-degree angle with Cemetery Hill and its ridge. This angle of fire would have given the Confederate artillery on July 2 a chance to enfilade the northernmost part of the whole Union line. Lee stated as much in his official report, when he referred to Longstreet gaining the Peach Orchard, or the "desired ground," from which his artillery could be "used to advantage in assailing the more elevated ground beyond, and thus enable us to reach the crest of the ridge."[10] The "ridge" Lee referred to could only be the northernmost section of Cemetery Ridge, including Cemetery Hill. Lee also must have been referring to Cemetery Hill and Ridge when he reported that "the enemy . . . had massed a large amount of artillery" upon that "ridge."[11] Little Round Top never had more than six to eight Union guns deployed on it—hardly a "large amount"—and thus could not have fit Lee's description.

The affirmed version of the battle mistakenly assumes that Lee's mention of the "more elevated ground beyond" refers to Little Round Top. Its proponents can accept that the "desired ground" in Lee's report was the Peach Orchard ridge, but to concede that Little Round Top was not Lee's ultimate objective, and therefore not a primary position for his artillery, is impossible. In order to show that Lee's "more elevated ground beyond," referred to Cemetery Ridge and Cemetery Hill beyond it, it is necessary at this point to explore the shortcomings of Little Round Top as an artillery position.

Little Round Top presented real problems for an artillery commander. At first glance, it appears that this hill offers a defender every possible advantage, commanding the field with its height and rugged terrain. Yet it was perhaps no better than the low portion of Cemetery Ridge, just north of it, for effective use of artillery. In fact, it might have been even worse because of the difficulty horses and drivers faced in attempting to place guns on top of it. Just as challenging would have been the task of hauling up ammunition. Reflecting on that difficulty, Lt. Benjamin F. Rittenhouse of Battery D, 5th U.S. Artillery, V Corps, later recounted: "Last May a young

Copse
of Trees

Ziegler's
Grove

Woods on
Southern edge
of Evergreen
Cemetery

A view from the north side of Little Round Top looking north to Cemetery Hill—
from one high point to another. This image was taken by Mathew Brady and
Company, around July 15, 1863, just twelve days after the battle. Observe the
openness of the terrain immediately below Little Round Top (in the foreground)
and how low a bottom it is compared to Little Round Top and Cemetery Hill (in
the background). Also note the prominence of Ziegler's Grove in comparison with
Bachelder's "copse of trees" as a terrain feature. Finally, note how the terrain
gradually rises to Cemetery Hill from the left, in front, and from the right.

artillery officer, who had just been on the [Little Round] Top, asked me how we got up there; I told him it was during the battle when everything was red hot, that the battery was ordered to the point, and that we went there at a trot, each man and horse trying to pull the whole battery by himself. In less time than it takes to tell it, four guns were on the crest, where a rider would hardly go today."[12]

The steepness of Little Round Top created another challenge for the placement of artillery. Because of the precipitous nature of the crest, guns firing from the hilltop would be effective only at long range. The barrels of the guns could not be depressed far enough to defend an area closer to Little Round Top unless canister was used, which was the option pursued by Captain Gibbs and his Ohio battery. A related problem was that to defend the hill, gunners would be forced to aim their guns down toward their own infantry.

Once the guns finally made it to the top of the hill, they encountered further problems. There are few level spaces at the crest, and the rocks covering it allowed little room for the guns to recoil.[13] If several cannons were pulled to the top, where would the numerous caissons of ammunition be kept, and how could the necessary spacing of several yards between guns and caissons be maintained? The steep eastern face of Little Round Top was wooded, covered with crags and boulders, and navigable only by a limited number of treacherous trails. How could the guns be withdrawn with speed and efficiency if the enemy seriously threatened to take the hill?

For all these reasons, Little Round Top was, in fact, as poor an artillery position as that low-lying section of Cemetery Ridge directly below and to the north of it. The ideal artillery platform was a ridge that offered a gradual rise, like the one at the Peach Orchard. It therefore made perfect sense for Lee to refer to the Peach Orchard ridge as "desired ground," and it stood to reason that Sickles, who commanded the Union III Corps in the hollow directly below and due east of that ridge, should have been very uneasy about his position on the morning of July 2.

CHAPTER 4

Why Little Round Top Was Not Lee's Objective

To state that Little Round Top was *not* the objective of the Confederate high command directly contradicts the affirmed version of the battle. The established scenario asserts that Longstreet was ordered to find the Union flank and drive it eastward, overtake Little Round Top, and then fire down on his opponent's flank from the vantage point of the towering hill. The accepted interpretation further argues that the Confederates planned to sever Union supply and communication lines several hundred yards east of the hill, at the Taneytown Road. Because this version of the story is so deeply entrenched, most historians presume that Lee saw the same merit in occupying Little Round Top as did the hill's postwar advocates such as Gen. Gouverneur K. Warren, Gen. Samuel Wiley Crawford, and Col. Joshua Chamberlain. But Lee's actions clearly illustrate that he did not see that hill as paramount to his plan of attack.

Lee's official report contains the evidence that he had a much greater interest in pushing Federal infantry northeast toward Cemetery Hill rather than east toward Little Round Top. On July 31, 1863, the general reported that "[Longstreet] was directed to endeavor to carry this position . . . crest of the ridge . . . while General Ewell attacked directly the high ground on the enemy's right."[1] The key phrase, alluding to an oblique order of battle aimed from the Confederate right toward Cemetery Hill, is: "*while General Ewell attacked directly.*" The last two words are most revealing, as they suggest that, unlike Ewell, Longstreet was ordered to attack indirectly. This assumption makes sense, considering that Longstreet would have had to attack indirectly in order to converge with Ewell, whose corps was on the Confederate left. A direct attack by Longstreet would have sent him due east, on a solo mission, pushing away from the rest of the Confederate army, grossly overextending an already exterior battle line. It is clear that in his July 2 orders, Lee intended for an indirect attack by Longstreet across A. P. Hill's Third Corps front to converge with a direct attack by Ewell, intersecting in the vicinity of Cemetery Hill.

Other key words in Lee's report point to an infantry assault aimed at a target other than Little Round Top. Striving to reach "the crest of the ridge" was one such phrase Lee used to describe the objective for Longstreet's attack, and he said this "ridge" was "massed [with] a large amount of artillery."[2] As students of the battle will attest, the vast majority of Union artillery pieces were positioned on Cemetery Hill, East Cemetery Hill, and Cemetery Ridge. Little Round Top was barren of artillery until around 5 P.M. on July 2—one and a half hours after the Confederate artillery bombardment started against the Union left.

Lee's after-action report of January 1864 provides more direct evidence that he wanted Longstreet to push more north than east and skirt past Little Round Top. In the report, he remarked that "Longstreet was directed to place the divisions of McLaws and Hood on the right of [A. P.] Hill, partially enveloping the enemy's left, which he was to drive in."[3] If Lee's intention had, in fact, been to capture Little Round Top, he would have said *fully* enveloping the enemy's left rather than "partially."

Further proof surfaces later in the same report, when Lee chastises Longstreet for having his operation "embarrassed [and] delayed by a force occupying the high, rocky hills on the enemy's extreme left, from which his troops could be attacked in reverse as they advanced."[4] How could this Union force, located on the "high, rocky hills" (a clear reference to the Round Tops), have attacked Longstreet's troops "in reverse" (from behind) unless the Confederate plans were to march north, staying just west of and passing by these "rocky hills"?

More proof of Lee's true intentions for Longstreet can be found in one of the most dramatic personal encounters of the July 2 battle: the clash between Longstreet and his subordinate divisional commander, Maj. Gen. John Bell Hood, popularly known as "Hood's Protest." The substance of the confrontation revolved around Longstreet's order that Hood attack the Union left flank on the afternoon of July 2. Hood was told to take his division and attack "up the Emmitsburg Road"[5]—that is to say, northeast, straight toward Cemetery Hill—and to let his "left rest on the Emmitsburg pike" as he advanced, to maintain his direction.[6]

Hood's objections to the order stemmed from information he received from a scouting party he had sent out to the area of the Round Tops, to the right of the location specified in his order. The scouts reported that Big Round Top was "unoccupied" and that "an open farm road around it led to unguarded supply trains and hospitals."[7] From this intelligence, Hood surmised that a wide, circuitous attack to the right, against the back side of the Round Tops, was feasible, even preferable. If he did not adopt this course, however, and agreed to attack the Union forces directly, Hood's scouts warned of the "immense boulders . . . narrow openings [and a] rocky precipice" that would "scatter" his men during the assault.[8]

As Hood reflected on the situation, it seems that he was overtaken by a slight hysteria. His knowledge of the Federal line, perhaps extending east to Little Round Top, caused him to imagine Union troops "easily repel[ling] our attack by merely throwing and rolling stones down the mountain side as we approached."[9] What was not imaginary, however, was the potential flank fire he feared he would encounter from any Federals occupying that rocky hill. If his troops had stayed on course, adhering strictly to the Emmitsburg Road, they would have passed just west of Little Round Top, with their right flank exposed to any troops posted there.

With the intelligence gathered from his scouts, Hood approached Longstreet, First Corps commander, and requested permission to carry out his circuitous flank attack to the far right, presumably against the eastern portion of Little Round Top. Hood made his request a total of three times, each time receiving the answer no. After each of his pleas had failed, including his attempts to have one of his brigade commanders, Brig. Gen. Evander M. Law, second his points, Hood finally acquiesced to his orders.

It is important to point out, however, that Hood did not scout the area himself, nor did he accompany his troops there, because of a crippling wound to his arm. He could only imagine the topography of the Round Tops and beyond, and hypothesize about where an alternative attack might take place. In a letter to Longstreet written in 1875, Hood claimed that he knew Little Round Top was the key to victory, and that his plan to take it from the reverse side would have worked. Twelve years after the battle, Hood had the luxury of falling back on the affirmed version of the battle that was already taking shape.[10]

Unfortunately, Hood's famous protest has become mired in the controversy of the Lee versus Longstreet feud, in which Longstreet advocates place Lee in Longstreet's company and even nearby during the July 2 meeting with Hood, thereby making Lee totally responsible for not seeing the value of Little Round Top. Lee supporters, on the other hand, view Longstreet as the villain: a man bent on sabotaging Confederate efforts because Lee had ignored his ideas. They believe that Longstreet rigidly stuck to Lee's plans, which were suited only for implementation against the Union army's position during the morning. And when Longstreet realized, as did one of his brigade commanders, General Kershaw, that the enemy's line was "extending to and upon the rocky mountain [Little Round Top] to [the Union] left far beyond the point at which his flank was supposed to rest,"[11] he maintained the original orders just to spite Lee.

Such degenerative debates over which of the two generals was at fault in denying Hood the option of swinging southeast of Little Round Top totally miss the point. The essence of Hood's objection strikes at the heart of something far more fundamental: Lee's real plan for Longstreet on July 2. That plan was for the Confederate right wing to attack the Union troops "up the Emmitsburg Road," in an oblique fashion, thereby rolling up Union lines to Cemetery Hill.

Lee's plan did not involve marching around Little Round Top under any circumstances, whether tactical or strategic, and Longstreet was well aware of that fact long before Hood's proposal. In fact, Longstreet's original strategy, which he had proposed to Lee the day before, had been to march the entire Confederate army around the Union flank, thus placing the Army of Northern Virginia between Meade's army and Washington, D.C. The logic of this strategy was that Meade might have been pressured to attack the defending Confederates, who perhaps could have obtained high ground and constructed entrenchments somewhere closer to Washington. But ultimately, Lee had rebutted that idea the previous evening; when Hood made his "protest" to Longstreet, it must have borne a familiar ring.

The point here is that Longstreet knew, prior to Hood's protest, that Lee was not interested in pursuing a circuitous march around the Union left, whether the march involved merely Hood's division or the entire army. If Lee had been interested in cutting off Union supplies southeast of Round Top at the Taneytown Road, he would have approved Longstreet's ambitious strategic maneuver in that direction the evening before.

All controversy aside, on a tactical level, Hood's proposal of moving around Little Round Top was simply a bad idea. From General Lee's perspective, the folly of a tactical swing beyond Little Round Top lay in the disadvantages of fighting on such a wide front. Lee's army was already stretched beyond its limits to turn the Union left at Little Round Top, especially in the late afternoon of July 2, when Hood made his protest.

A closer inspection of the deployment and state of Lee's whole army bears this out. First, Ewell's Second Corps, which faced the Union right flank, was spread out east-west, from Benner's Hill and the Hanover Road, across the town, and over to Seminary Ridge. In other words, Ewell was stretched around the entire curvature of the Union salient. A. P. Hill's Third Corps, which was deployed to Ewell's right, along Seminary Ridge, covered a smaller radius but had other problems. His corps was at a disadvantage because two of his three divisions had been battered by fighting on July 1. Although Hill had less total frontage to cover than Ewell, only Anderson's division was any real threat to the Union center that day. The Third Corps was mostly to play the role of decoy: Hill was "ordered to threaten the enemy's center, to prevent reinforcements being drawn to either wing, and co-operate with his right division in Longstreet's attack."[12]

Only Longstreet's First Corps was undamaged after the first day's battle, and only his line was tight enough in frontage to make an impact. Yet even so, the 13,000 men he had available were still in jeopardy of being stretched too thin, because not all of the corps' divisions had arrived. Maj. Gen. George E. Pickett's division did not reach the outskirts of Gettysburg until around 6 P.M. and would therefore not be available until the next morning at the earliest.

With this in mind, Lee knew that if Hood's division left the Emmitsburg Road and veered east to "march through an open woodland pasture around Round Top and assault the enemy in flank and rear," then part of his force would become detached, and the overall assault would not pack the necessary punch.[13] Moreover, Lee's entire line would be vulnerable, especially A. P. Hill's segment at the center. Simply put, for Longstreet to attack east of Little Round Top was to further stretch out a greatly overextended Army of Northern Virginia battle line, which already covered twice the distance of its opponent's. Even if Hood's division did capture Little Round Top and manage to hold on to it, the men could not have stayed there while the rest of Lee's army was chasing a different goal—the northern portion of Cemetery Ridge and Cemetery Hill.

If the Federal position on Little Round Top had indeed been overrun, Union artillery pieces would have been stranded. It is likely that the various chiefs of each section (two cannon per section) would have spiked their guns' priming holes and carried the loading implements away, rendering each piece useless for the invaders. This would have left part of Hood's division atop Little Round Top, isolated from the rest of the fight. Eventually the Confederate position there would have been untenable, as the brunt of an entire fresh Union VI Corps could have swept over them, if Meade so desired. Attacking Little Round Top could not have been a pre-planned Confederate objective on July 2, for either Longstreet or Lee, because taking it gained very little. A sustained Confederate occupation of that hill would only have brought Hood's division to a tactical dead end, while the rest of the Confederate army attempted to converge northeast.

CHAPTER 5

Lee's Plan to
Converge His Forces

L ee's army was spread nearly to the limit of its effectiveness. In order to
restore its strength, Lee needed to concentrate his army's numbers by
converging his separated corps. The two wings of his army, which consisted
of Ewell on the left and Longstreet on the right, would be required to advance together toward "a point of impact," where numerical superiority
could be brought to bear on a single spot in the enemy's line, and so overwhelm it. The salient protruding from Cemetery Hill provided just such a
point of impact. It was the bulwark of the Union line and an excellent
place to direct converging forces. It is clear that Lee wanted his flank corps
to come together, not to extend them in separate directions beyond their
means to reinforce one another—as believers of the affirmed event propose.

Lee's motivation for returning to this tactical principle may have been
grounded in his respect for a military manual popular among Civil War
generals at the time, *The Art of War*, another work by Baron Jomini. Jomini's work not only offers explanations for some of Lee's tactical decisions
at Gettysburg, but also provides the apparent framework for his battle plan
on July 2. In one section, for example, Jomini advised that a commanding
general who assumed the offensive should "endeavor in all his combina-
tions, whether deliberately arranged or adopted on the spur of the moment, to form a sound conclusion as to the important point of the
battlefield; . . . [while] not forgetting the direction in which strategy re-
quires him to operate. He will then give his attention and efforts to this

41

point, using a third of his force to keep the enemy in check or watch his movements, while throwing the other two-thirds upon the point the possession of which will insure him the victory."[1]

At Gettysburg, the "important point" toward which Lee "threw" his army was Cemetery Hill. On July 2, Longstreet and Ewell constituted the "two-thirds," while A. P. Hill represented the third of Lee's force "to keep the enemy in check or watch his movements."

Intertwined with this self-evident blueprint, Jomini put forth other formulas that Lee employed on July 2. For instance, Lee's hard dismissal of Longstreet's desire to march around Meade's left may have stemmed from Jomini's belief that the success of taking "detours" around an enemy's flank was usually doubtful, "since it depends upon such an accurate execution of carefully arranged plans as is rarely seen."[2]

Jomini also defined the terms that became fundamental to the way Lee proceeded in battle. He identified the only course a general could pursue when he had inherited exterior lines, as Lee had throughout Gettysburg. Jomini first defined exterior lines as those "formed by an army which operates at the same time on both flanks of the enemy,"[3] and then explained how a general could operate on these flanks in a decisive manner. To do so, he must manuever along "concentric lines of operations," combining the wings of his army that "depart from widely separated points and meet at the same point, either in advance of or behind the base [of the enemy]."[4] Lee obviously favored this tactic of "concentric lines" on July 2, when he ordered two of his own widely separated corps to converge on the same spot of the strategic salient at Cemetery Hill.

Lee used the same tactic not only at Gettysburg, but also for nearly every major tactically offensive battle he had previously conducted. At Chancellorsville, the battle immediately preceding Gettysburg, in May, Lee divided his force in the face of the enemy, sending Gen. "Stonewall" Jackson around the Union right to launch a surprise flank attack, while Lee himself remained south of the Federal army. The plan was for the two wings to converge in the area of the Chancellor house, and eventually they did. Had Jackson and subsequently A. P. Hill not been wounded, and had Union general Winfield Scott Hancock not instituted his retrograde maneuver to relieve the pressed Federal infantry, then Lee's army perhaps would have cut off the Federals' line of retreat to the Rappahannock River. And Lee would have achieved this with the execution of a pincerlike maneuver, very similar to the move he attempted with Longstreet and Ewell at Gettysburg on July 2. The tactical plan at Chancellorsville was a great gamble, but Lee believed it to be worth the risk.

Other examples of Lee concentrating his forces at a "point of impact" include both Second Manassas and the Seven Days' Battles around Richmond. Evidence of converging Confederate forces at Second Manassas in August 1862 is readily obvious. Union general John Pope was lured into the attack on the Confederate left flank held by Jackson, only to be ambushed by Longstreet, who fell in on Pope's committed troops. Lee, Longstreet, and Jackson executed a textbook pincer maneuver, nearly destroying Pope's Union forces.

Perhaps the Seven Days' Battles around Richmond in May and June 1862 provide the most extreme example of Lee's willingness to split his forces in the attempt to bring them together. Between Union general George B. McClellan and Richmond, Lee left a relatively small force of about 22,000 infantry to stop the Union army's advance on the Confederate capital. Meanwhile, Lee moved the bulk of his army, roughly 52,000 troops, northwest of McClellan, then moved across the Chickahominy River before landing on his enemy's right flank.

Dividing his forces this way was an exceedingly dangerous maneuver. Lee did this in front of a Federal army that consisted of nearly 100,000 men, taking a gamble well before McClellan developed his reputation for timidity. Not only did Lee divide his forces, but he also separated them without equity. Confederate general "Prince" John Magruder was entrusted with barely a third of the army with which to protect the most direct east-west route to Richmond. Conceivably, had Union intelligence detected this information, McClellan's 100,000 men could have rolled over Magruder into the Confederate capital. Moreover, Lee's greater force of 52,000 exposed its own left flank to Gen. Irvin McDowell's thousands who might have moved down from Fredericksburg. Although Lee relied on information contained in an intercepted Union dispatch predicting that McDowell would not assist McClellan, even the slightest risk of a change of Union plans could have led to the destruction of what came to be known as Lee's Army of Northern Virginia and the capture of Richmond. Yet Lee was willing to take that chance.

On July 2, 1863, Lee was willing once again to divide his forces in the face of the enemy and take the risk that they could fight their way through and converge. With two-thirds of A. P. Hill's corps temporarily disabled from the fighting on July 1, the maneuver was to be attempted by Longstreet on one flank and Ewell on the other. Longstreet was to make the main attack against the Union left, and when Ewell detected the approach of Longstreet's guns, according to Lee's report of January 1864, he was to make a "simultaneous demonstration" against the Union right, with the probability of converting this "into a real attack should opportunity offer."[5] A. P. Hill's forces were to pin down the Union center, while his one fresh division, under Anderson, was to assist Longstreet in rolling the Union battle line obliquely toward the "salient" of Cemetery Hill.

If all worked according to plan, Longstreet's corps would have un-hinged Sickles's III Corps line, which initially stretched from Devil's Den due west of Little Round Top to the Emmitsburg Road, and pushed it to-ward the northern end of Cemetery Ridge and the Hill itself, which would have most assuredly created an opportunity for Ewell to parlay his demon-stration into an all-out offensive. The "point of impact" was the salient of Cemetery Hill, and the actual offensive to be performed could be called a

---

OPPOSITE PAGE: A more detailed map of Lee's plan of attack for Long-street, Hill, and Ewell on Day 2 of the battle. The main focus of Lee's at-tack on Day 2 was to take the Peach Orchard. From the outset, the Confederates had planned to take this position in order to place artillery there to fire up Cemetery Ridge. Lee had thought that they could take the Peach Orchard without any fight, but Sickles's unexpected forward move-ment frustrated this goal. By moving forward, Sickles did gain a far superior artillery position, but he was also forced to cover 800 yards of additional geography, and thus overextended his line. Once Meade realized what Sickles had done, he sent in portions of the Union II, V, VI, and XII Corps to reinforce Sickles's line, swelling it from 9,500 to 30,000 men. With only 13,000 Confederate troops, Lee was outnumbered more than three to one. Meanwhile, Union troops positioned on Little Round Top caused Long-street to shift the focus of the attack to the east. Lee's line was already seven miles long and couldn't afford this diversion away from the planned attack "up the Emmitsburg Road." In the end, it is remarkable that Lee succeeded in taking the Peach Orchard, but only at the cost of thousands of lives and huge quantities of ammunition for a position that he had ini-tially planned to take without having to fire a shot. The end result of this was that when Pickett went in on Day 3, he did so with greatly reduced ar-tillery support stemming from the depletion of Confederate munitions.

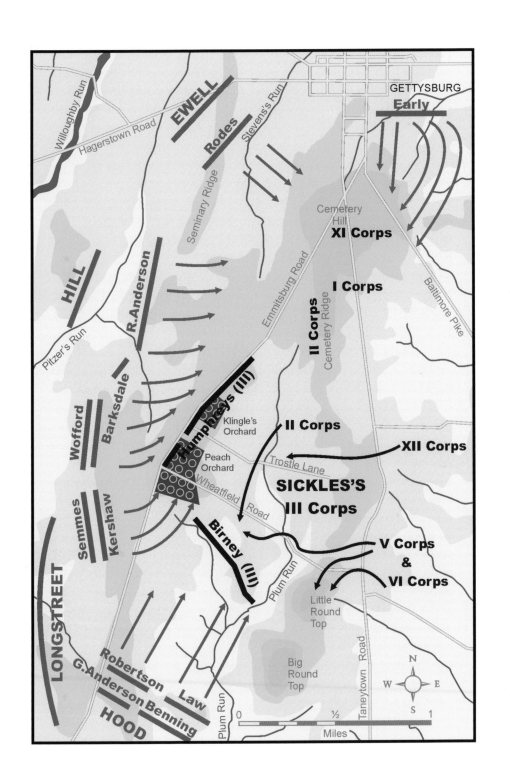

pincer or double envelopment. Once the separated wings of Lee's army converged, they would achieve maximum firepower, as the Union salient would take fire from its two sides and nose. Numbers would have come together in Lee's favor to overwhelm the most vulnerable point along the Union battle line, producing the very result demanded of an attack on a "point of impact."

Historians, who have operated until now within the framework of the affirmed version of the battle, have had trouble accepting Ewell's order to make a "simultaneous demonstration" on hearing Longstreet's guns, while he was also to look for an opportunity to develop it into a real attack. They take greater comfort in believing that Ewell was to participate in an all-out flank attack at the same time as Longstreet.

Longstreet's own postwar writings provide the main evidence for this affirmed interpretation. His article in *Battles and Leaders of the Civil War, 1884–1887,* entitled "Lee's Right Wing at Gettysburg," is one example. Frustrated, Longstreet stated: "Lee's orders had been that when my advance was made the Second Corps (Ewell) on his left should move and make a simultaneous attack. Ewell made no move at all until 8 o'clock at night after the heat of the battle was over."[6] Either Longstreet truly believed that Ewell was to engage in a synchronized push or, perhaps more deviously, he was trying to cover suspicions surrounding why his own attack did not begin until late in the afternoon, at 4 P.M. (Without daylight savings time and four standard time zones, darkness fell locally by 7:15 P.M. Dusk set in around 6:30 P.M.) In other words, Longstreet may have wanted Ewell to bear greater responsibility for the failure of the Confederate wings to converge, and therefore painted Ewell in a compromising light. Although this underhandedness is unthinkable to Longstreet devotees, he had set a precedent for such behavior after the battle of Seven Pines a year earlier, when he and Gen. Joseph E. Johnston conspired to cover their own shortcomings by offering Maj. Gen. Benjamin Huger as their scapegoat.[7]

A second source for the preoccupation of some historians with a simultaneous flank attack on July 2 draws on a much deeper issue of the history of the battle. The battle has long been interpreted from the Union standpoint, in which Union defenders are portrayed as fending off repeated Confederate offensives. From that perspective, the Union battle line from July 1 through July 3 has become one large area where a series of emergencies was addressed. Both Union veterans and historians through the years have emphasized individual locations where Union forces made their stand. Over the decades, these various positions have become enshrined and set apart. Each position, such as Little Round Top, Devil's Den, Wheatfield, Stony Hill, and even the Peach Orchard, has grown beyond a means to a Confederate end. Instead, each has become an end in itself: the sole objective of the battle.

The real intentions of the Confederate army do not fit with this approach. In the larger scheme, General Lee was not satisfied with capturing any of these hallowed spots in particular. All of these locations were significant as points where Lee's plans were hindered, but none of them would have stood alone in his overall plan. Instead, each was a stepping stone, not a shrine, in his greater tactical strategy. Each position was merely a checkpoint in Lee's mind (if that): He expected Longstreet's men to quickly pass through each of them en route to cracking the Union salient and capturing the key network of roads within.

The main point here in regard to how timely Ewell's attack should have been is that the battle's historiography has been so characterized by small unit actions from the Union perspective that the broader Confederate strategy has remained beside the point. Ewell's offensive on July 2 has been important only as it pertained to the Union-occupied areas of Culp's Hill, East Cemetery Hill, and Cemetery Hill. To this end, a simultaneous attack against the Union flanks is the extent to which Union veterans and their unit historians wanted to address Confederate strategy.[8] And since the Union story line originally prevailed, the real specifics of Confederate tactical strategy for July 2, 1863, have become secondary.

That Ewell and Longstreet were working together to "crack the nut" at the bulwark of the Union line, with Longstreet bearing the brunt of the attack, has become lost in the shuffle of Federal unit histories. Understandably, Union veterans never would have found it comfortable to accept that General Lee's greater goal lay beyond most of the enshrined areas. Perhaps this is beside the point, though. Truthfully, most Union veterans were not concerned with learning details of Confederate strategy.[9]

So in reality, Longstreet was to initiate the Confederate offensive against the Union left on July 2, while Ewell made a "simultaneous demonstration" until the "opportunity" for a real attack presented itself. If Longstreet had been successful in rolling up Union forces toward Cemetery Hill, then Ewell would have been presented with a clear and obvious opportunity. The fact that Longstreet was not able to push his Union opposition back toward Cemetery Hill explains why Ewell had such great difficulty in finding an opening for a real attack.

CHAPTER 6

Why Lee Failed
on Day Two

What went wrong, then, with Confederate tactics on July 2? Why did Longstreet's attack not proceed "up the Emmitsburg Road" as planned? A closer analysis points to several specific failures in the execution of Confederate tactical strategy.

The first breakdown lay in the lateness of the offensive against the Union left. This criticism should not be interpreted as a condemnation of either Lee or Longstreet; it is simply a statement of fact. An oblique strike along the Emmitsburg Road would have been far more effective had it been executed before the remainder of Meade's army arrived at Gettysburg. When Lee was devising his plan of attack during the early morning of July 2 (or perhaps in rudimentary form the night before), Meade's forces were not concentrated on the battlefield. Both the Union VI Corps under Sedgwick and the artillery reserve were in transit, while Sickles's III Corps and Sykes's V Corps were still moving into position. Although Lee could not have known these specifics, he did comprehend that the sooner he attacked, the better his chances to strike a foe at less than full strength.

But what specifics of the Union position did Lee in fact know? General Hunt believed he knew the answer to that question. The chief of Meade's artillery was quite observant on this point. He surmised that Lee's scouts had informed him that the Union left ended along Cemetery Ridge, with only a small contingent of Federals holding a position in advance at the Peach Orchard.[1] It was with this information, obtained in the early morning, that Lee formulated his plan.

Hunt was probably not far off in his estimation of Lee's knowledge. As early as 4 A.M., Lee and Longstreet had sent out scouts to investigate the Union left. The most notable of these was Capt. Samuel Johnston, who surveyed much of the area from the Peach Orchard around to Warfield Ridge and down to Houck's Ridge, and possibly as far east as the Round Tops. It has generally been a mystery how Johnston could have made it onto Little Round Top as he claimed, further complicated by the fact that his descriptions do not match what he should have seen from there.

However far east Johnston did go, it seemed to be farther than Lee was expecting. Lee's reaction of surprise that Johnston had covered so much ground was caused by the fact that the Round Tops did not figure in his plan.[2] Perhaps more important for the purposes of this argument, Johnston identified only a very small Union presence along the southernmost portions of Cemetery Ridge. He did not detect Sickles's III Corps or Buford's cavalry, whose position should have been easily observed. All in all, Hunt's assessment of Lee's knowledge seems intuitively correct.

What should be remembered here is that Lee's tactical plans for July 2 were originally based on the belief that the Federal presence in the Peach Orchard was minimal. It was a Union flank placed out in the air, with the nearest support to the northeast, along the middle and southern portions of Cemetery Ridge. A Confederate oblique attack following the Emmitsburg Road, with Maj. Gen. Lafayette McLaws's division sweeping through the orchard and joining Hood, whose right flank would touch down at Cemetery Ridge, seemed the perfect call. Had the attack been made earlier in the day, this scenario could have played out successfully, giving Lee the pivotal victory he so desired. As it turned out, however, the attack was made around 4 P.M., by which time Union troops were better prepared. To this point, Maj. Gen. Jubal A. Early, who commanded a division in Ewell's corps, summarized: "The objection which General Hood made in regard to attacking up the Emmitsburg road, would not have existed in the morning or forenoon, because the Round Tops were not then occupied, and it was the delay in the attack that produced the difficulty he mentions."[3]

Even if an earlier attack from Lee's right wing had occurred, the presence of Sickles's III Corps presented real problems. Lee did not account for their presence—either along Cemetery Ridge, where Meade presupposed them to be, or in the elaborate, protruding position through the Peach Orchard that developed—in his order for the Emmitsburg Road attack. The unexpected presence of Sickles, in any form, lay at the heart of the second reason why Lee's general plan for July 2 only "partially succeeded."[4]

Meade had ordered Sickles to remain along the southernmost part of Cemetery Ridge, down in the low bottom of Plum Run Valley, where Brig. Gen. John W. Geary's division of XII Corps had been the night before. If Sickles's position matched that of Geary, as Meade's orders seemed to call for, his corps would have stretched from the George Weikert farm, on his right, to the northern slope of Little Round Top, on his left. In this scenario, Sickles could have threatened the right flank of a Confederate attack "up the Emmitsburg Road." If Longstreet had chosen to bypass the Federal III Corps position there, en route to striking the more northerly parts of Cemetery Ridge and Cemetery Hill, then Sickles could have attacked Longstreet from behind. From reading Lee's official report, it is obvious that Longstreet was concerned about being "attacked in reverse" (from behind) along that part of the Federal line on July 2.[5] He was indeed worried about the extension of the Federal left wing that he could not measure.

Although this sequence of events is perhaps closer to what Meade had envisioned, it is not in fact what happened. What Sickles actually did was possibly even more disruptive to Lee's plan. Understandably, to make a claim such as this is heresy to believers of the affirmed event, but it is not a claim without merit. Before Sickles advanced to the Peach Orchard, his III Corps was deployed along the section of Cemetery Ridge with the poorest terrain, "where it [was] gradually diminishing in elevation."[6] There was a rocky ridge behind, or east of, this portion of diminished ground that was heavily wooded, featuring perhaps three isolated woodlots, but the ground there was covered with crags and boulders, preventing easy deployment of artillery. The ground immediately west of this rocky ridge and below it was cleared, but very low and wet, making it equally undesirable for artillery placement.

The fields directly south of the George Weikert farm still become very wet and soft in the spring and summer months. Drainage south from Cemetery Ridge, east from the Peach Orchard ridge, west from the aforementioned ridge, and north from Little Round Top converges to make those fields south of the present Pennsylvania Memorial tricky even for modern hikers and horseback riders. This is especially the case during rainy seasons, when basement floods are not uncommon at the George Weikert house. Today, however, acres of modern tree growth, along with the trees'

The "low bottom," where drainage from Little Round Top (to the south), Emmitsburg Road ridge (to the west), and Cemetery Ridge (to the north) settles. Before Maj. Gen. John Sedgwick's VI Corps arrived, Sickles's III Corps had to deal with this marshy ground alone. To the right, and in the foreground is the headquarters monument for Sedgwick's VI Corps. The woods, in the left background, are largely postwar. Acres of relatively modern woods on that part of the field today absorb much of the drainage that Sickles had to contend with in July 1863. The park's general management plan calls for the gradual restoration of this ground to its original appearance. PHOTOGRAPH BY LISA HARMAN

mature root systems, absorb much of the groundwater. There would have been a much greater quantity in 1863, when the III Corps had to contend with soft ground, standing puddles, and a wider Plum Run.

Overall, there was much truth to Sickles's belief that "from Hancock's [II Corps] line to Round Top was a line through swale morass, swamp, boulders, and forest and tangled undergrowth, unfit for infantry, [and] impracticable for artillery."[7] Consequently, artillery there would be severely hampered, leaving Sickles's officers and men without sufficient support. Compounding the problem was the rocky, steep, and almost inaccessible nature of Little Round Top. If anything, this precipice was even less advantageous for Sickles's guns.

Conversely, Longstreet's artillery would have held higher ground and could have shot down on that diminished part of Cemetery Ridge from the vicinity of the Peach Orchard. Conceivably, Sickles's fears of a repeat of the circumstances of Hazel Grove at Chancellorsville could have been realized. Indeed, occupation of the orchard presented such a distinct advantage that it is not hard to imagine disastrous consequences for Sickles's corps, which could have returned only slight artillery fire, had it fallen under the Confederate guns. Under these circumstances, Sickles would have had to charge uphill into the Confederate batteries in an attempt to silence them. Sickles firmly held that his original position was so insufficient that it was "hopelessly dominated by the ridge in front [along Emmitsburg Road] which I would have surrendered to Lee without a blow. . . . I would have had no positions whatever for my own artillery over one-half my line, and would have surrendered to Lee the positions for his artillery, which he states in his official report it was the object of his movement to gain."[8]

Sickles was absolutely correct in his assumption that Lee desired that ground for artillery. In fact, the Peach Orchard was the only ground on the Union left flank that Lee specified as an objective. It is conceivable, therefore, that Sickles's fears of a one-sided artillery barrage could have been realized had he remained in his original position. The Confederate attack that would have followed can only be speculated on, but perhaps McLaws's division would have supported batteries in the Peach Orchard during their artillery bombardment of the III Corps line, while Hood's division, the other half of Longstreet's corps then available, along with Anderson's division of A. P. Hill's corps, might have attacked toward northern Cemetery Ridge and Cemetery Hill. Attacking earlier than was actually done probably would have presented Ewell with a conspicuous opportunity to enter the fight at the other flank.

Much of this remains speculation because of Sickles's forward movement, which occurred shortly after noon on July 2. By moving out from the hollow that is Plum Run Valley, he forced Lee to fight it out on a line far south of the Confederate objective—the salient at Cemetery Hill. Sickles forced Lee to struggle for possession of the Peach Orchard, so essential as an artillery platform from which to enfilade the Cemetery Ridge position. The chief of Union artillery, General Hunt, asserted: "The salient line [into the orchard] proposed by General Sickles was the only one on the field from which we could have passed from the defensive to the offensive with a prospect of decisive results."[9]

A view from the Longstreet Tower, along West Confederate Avenue, looking toward the Peach Orchard, which Lee reported to be "desired ground." At the time of the battle, the orchard would have extended to the far left of the photograph, where it would have connected with Klingle's Apple Orchard. Much of the thick wooded area to the left of the barn, known as Codori thicket, would not have been there during the battle. Without these woods, there would have been a clearer view of that portion of Cemetery Ridge. PHOTOGRAPH BY LISA HARMAN

In a practical sense, Sickles's movement forward toward the orchard forced Meade to attend to events on his left flank. Meade, who had been active throughout the morning inspecting the northern part of the Union line from Culp's Hill past Cemetery Hill to Cemetery Ridge, had not displayed the same diligence or interest in personally inspecting positions on the Union left. Either because of his antipathy toward Sickles or because he believed the real threat to his line existed around the Cemetery Hill salient, Meade merely sent emissaries to survey the position of the III Corps. Meade had also shown an interest in advancing the Union V and XII Corps from the Baltimore Pike northeasterly across Rock Creek to Wolf Hill, and perhaps as far as Benner's Hill. Up until noon of July 2, he had considered such an offensive maneuver from his right flank. In any case, Meade was preoccupied with his right and center for most of July 2.

It is true that Sickles liberally interpreted Meade's orders by moving his troops forward. But he had just cause for doing so. The Confederate threat was too real from that sector, and the original Union position too inadequate, for Sickles to act conventionally. If he did not move forward and seize the Peach Orchard, then his enemy would have done so, leaving much of the Union II Corps, then posted on his right along Cemetery Ridge, to suffer a severe enfilading artillery fire. Moreover, Confederate fire from the Peach Orchard probably would have aided Ewell's corps on the far left, particularly Maj. J. W. Latimer's artillery battalion on Benner's Hill, east of town, which suffered heavy losses from the Union guns on Cemetery Hill. Latimer's guns might not have been destroyed had Col. Edward Porter Alexander's Confederate artillery battalion been able to respond from the Peach Orchard around 3:30 P.M. that day. Also, the citadel of Union guns on Cemetery Hill would have come under bombardment simultaneously from all three Confederate corps, aimed from four directions. Concentric artillery fire there might have proved too much for the Union defenders.

This same convergence of artillery fire would be attempted again on July 3, but by then Latimer's guns on Benner's Hill were greatly reduced in numbers and disappointing in their effectiveness. Overall, there were far-reaching consequences in forfeiting the Peach Orchard to the Confederates on July 2.

A third reason for Lee's failure on July 2 was the wounding of General Hood at the outset of the attack when a shell burst above him, driving a fragment into his left arm. It was the temporary break in leadership caused by Hood's early exit from the action that allowed the course of the attack to drift right, rather than up the Emmitsburg Road. Hood's replacement, Brig. Gen. Evander M. Law, did not immediately assume command, leaving a power vacuum and lack of direction for the troops. In the absence of overall control, decision making devolved to subordinate unit commanders.

Finding themselves "without a leader and ignorant of where the enemy [was]," regimental commanders such as those in Law's own brigade made adjustments to the battle line as they advanced.[10] Col. William C. Oates of the 15th Alabama was one such officer. His regiment, originally third from the right flank of the army, first encountered Col. Hiram Berdan's Union sharpshooters at the John Slyder farm, immediately south and west of Big Round Top and south of Devil's Den. As he engaged them, the sharpshooters fell back northeasterly, up and over Big Round Top, disappearing and reappearing "as if commanded by a magician."[11] Their diagonal withdrawal lured the Alabamians in that direction. Colonel Oates feared that if he did not pursue their skirmish line, he would leave them and some unknown Union force, which perhaps they were screening, in his rear. He therefore decided to follow Berdan's course. The Alabama colonel became so single-minded in pursuing the Union skirmish line farther to his right that he failed to obey an order from Law to "left-wheel" and get back on track because he was "rapidly advancing up the mountain."[12] As Longstreet remembered, "Hood's line was extended to the right to protect its flank from the sweeping fire of the large bodies of troops that were posted on Round Top."[13]

The altered course the Alabama regiments pursued profoundly affected the course of Hood's entire line. First, Brig. Gen. J. B. Robertson's Texas Brigade, to the left of Law, found it impossible to stay connected with the Emmitsburg Road and still remain connected with the wayward Alabamians. As Robertson explained: "I was ordered to keep my right well closed on Brigadier-General Law's left, and to let my left rest on the Emmitsburg pike. I had advanced but a short distance when I discovered that my brigade would not fill the space between General Law's left and the pike named."[14]

Robertson's failure to close up created a large gap in the middle of the Confederate line. Interestingly, the battle line divided somewhat unconventionally, with Robertson's two right regiments, the 5th and 4th Texas, clinging to the three left regiments of Law, the 4th, 47th, and 15th Alabama. Consequently, the breach actually occurred within Robertson's brigade, separating his two left regiments by as much as 200 yards from his two right ones. The left regiments, the 3rd Arkansas and 1st Texas, entered Rose Woods and the western portion of the "Triangular Field," a triangle of three stone walls adjacent to Devil's Den, while the 5th and 4th Texas, to the right, traversed the western slope of Big Round Top.

To compensate for this, General Law shifted the two right regiments of his brigade, the 44th and 48th Alabama, into the fissure of the line, placing them geographically in lower Plum Run Valley and lower Devil's Den. Quite by good fortune for the Confederates, their ruptured line became further strengthened with the arrival of Brig. Gen. Henry L. Benning's Georgia Brigade, which mistakenly followed Robertson to that area. Benning plainly stipulated, "In the attack my brigade would follow Law's Brigade at the distance of about 400 yards."[15] Once the attack began, however, a significant mix-up occurred "due to a wood concealing from me most of Law's Brigade," said Benning. "The part of [the assaulting line] in our front I took to be Law's Brigade, and so I followed it. In truth, it was Robertson's, Law's being farther to the right."[16] One might add (because it certainly is implied) that when Benning lost sight of Law's brigade, he directed his troops toward where Law was originally intended to go, which was to the west of, and skirting past, Little Round Top.

As for the left of Hood's division, which was intended to remain attached to the Emmitsburg Road, its course drifted more easterly than northerly, with respect to the undertow of the Union skirmish line, which drew Law's brigade diagonally over Big Round Top, toward its doom. Faced with the realization that he could not both cleave to the Emmitsburg Road and adhere to Law, Robertson "abandoned the pike, and closed on General Law's left."[17] Simply stated, Hood's division could not attack Little Round Top and remain attached to the Emmitsburg Road. The divisional line was not long enough. Said Longstreet, "These . . . movements of extension so drew my forces out, that I found myself attacking Cemetery Hill with a single line of battle against no less than fifty thousand troops."[18] Considering that Longstreet's task was to drive the Union line in all the way to Cemetery Hill, his estimate of 50,000 opposing troops was probably accurate.

The magnetic pull of Little Round Top forced more alterations. With Hood's left drifting east away from the Peach Orchard, which was the real "desired ground," tactical adjustments became mandatory. Here Maj. Gen. Lafayette McLaws's division entered the plan. This was not a surprise, though. Robertson indicated in his report that McLaws's participation in the advance had already been preestablished, a fact that influenced him in the decision to depart from the Emmitsburg Road. Robertson recalled that there was an "understanding before the action commenced that the attack on our part was to be general, and that the force of General McLaws was to advance simultaneously with us on my immediate left."[19]

Specifically, McLaws's two lead brigades, under Brig. Gen. Joseph B. Kershaw and Brig. Gen. William Barksdale, were to move out from their concealed position, behind a stone wall that was roughly parallel to the Emmitsburg Road, then dress right and wheel left, "swinging around toward the Peach Orchard."[20] Kershaw, who was on the right, would wheel left and try to connect on his right with Brig. Gen. George "Tiege" Anderson's support brigade, of Hood's division, at the western edge of the Wheatfield, while Barksdale was to move out, keeping on Kershaw's left, to reconnect the Confederate line with the Emmitsburg Road. Kershaw reinforced Robertson's understanding that the attack would be general when he noted: "I was directed to commence the attack so soon as General Hood became engaged, swinging around toward the peach orchard, and at the same time establishing connection with Hood on my right, and cooperating with him. . . . Barksdale would move with me and conform to my movement."[21]

Adding more credence to the notion that the attack was to proceed following the Emmitsburg Road, Kershaw later wrote, "It was understood he [Hood] was to sweep down the enemy's line in a direction perpendicular (T) to our then line of battle."[22] Consistent with this was Lee's clash with Longstreet in the early morning of July 2, over where McLaws's division should eventually be placed in relation to the Union left:

> Lee pointed out to McLaws, on the map, the position on the Emmitsburg road, at right angles to that near the peach orchard, that he desired him to occupy, telling him to gain that, if possible without being seen by the enemy. Longstreet interposed, directing McLaws to place his line parallel to the turnpike. Lee promptly made reply: "No, General, no; I want his position perpendicular to the Emmitsburg road," thus clearly indicating his design to move squarely upon the Federal left.[23]

Ultimately McLaws was to aid Hood, as they were expected to "fall on the left flank of the Federal line and force it toward Gettysburg," and not toward the Taneytown Road, as some might think.[24]

Had these modifications been properly executed, then an "attack up the Emmitsburg Road" could perhaps have been restored to order. This was not to be, however, as Barksdale and his supporting brigade under Brig. Gen. William T. Wofford failed to move in unison with Kershaw and his support brigade under Brig. Gen. Paul J. Semmes. Perhaps due to Longstreet's direct involvement, Kershaw had moved almost to the Emmitsburg Road before Barksdale's men rose to the drums and "beat [of] assembly."[25]

The belated movement and lack of coordination had serious ramifications for Kershaw's South Carolinians as they attempted to cover the same frontage meant for both Kershaw's and Barksdale's brigades. Even with direct support from Semmes, the right half of Kershaw's brigade became mired in one fight along the western border of the Wheatfield, while his left futilely faced in a different direction to attack the Peach Orchard. His fight on two separate fronts became overextended, yet it was somehow maintained until a false order reached his left regiments at the orchard. Mistakenly interpreted, the order seemed to call for all of Kershaw's brigade to shift right, away from the orchard. Not only did Kershaw's left regiments forfeit what little success they had gained, but they also suffered severely in their withdrawal.

Barksdale began his attack belatedly, yet he still successfully dislodged the Federal position at the Peach Orchard, even pushing Brig. Gen. Charles K. Graham's Federal brigade back to the northeast, closely following the predetermined course of the Emmitsburg Road. Because of Barksdale's poor coordination with Kershaw, however, the latter's brigade was reduced in number and greatly weakened, and McLaws's division was ultimately robbed of the impact that all four of its brigades might have made together. This breakdown within the division, coupled with Hood's wounding and the confusion that followed, had shifted the course of the attack more toward Little Round Top and away from the objectives set forth in the original orders issued by Lee.

Another reason for the failure of Lee's plan for July 2 was General Meade's committal of roughly 20,000 troops to the Union left flank to bolster Sickles's III Corps line. Although Sickles did grasp the importance of the Peach Orchard as a preferred artillery position, the forward movement of his troops away from the marshy hollow and rugged ridges created new vulnerabilities.

Sickles's decision not to occupy Little Round Top was not necessarily the biggest concern. His bigger weakness in moving forward to the Emmitsburg Road was the overextended nature of his line. By advancing the III Corps, he formed a salient, thus stretching 9,500 Union soldiers across a wide arch. As with other salients, the corps sacrificed its depth in expanding its frontage, while presenting a battle line that was only at half strength on either side, able merely to produce dispersed, rather than convergent, fire. Consequently, there were gaps throughout his line, creating a position that could not be maintained without help from other Union corps. But before Sickles is ultimately condemned, two things should be remembered: First, if Sickles is to be criticized for creating a salient position, then Meade also must be judged on that point, as the entire Union fishhook line was a salient position. Second, if left unaided in his former position, Sickles would have been even more prone to disaster. Indeed, Sickles was in an unenviable position.

Unfortunately for Lee and Longstreet, Meade reinforced Sickles's III Corps substantially by sending in elements of the V, II, XII, and eventually VI Corps. It was Brig. Gen. John C. Caldwell's division of Hancock's II Corps that thwarted Anderson's Georgia Brigade as well as Kershaw's men in the area of the Wheatfield and Stony Ridge. Had not that Union division been sent in at that particular moment, and had the brigades of Barksdale and Wofford immediately moved out alongside Kershaw and Semmes, as they had been ordered to do, it is possible to imagine an immediate and sweeping dislodgment of the Union line, from the Peach Orchard to Devil's Den, and the realization of an oblique attack "up the Emmitsburg Road."

There is another obstacle to imagining such Confederate success, however, as serious students of the battle understand. Elements of Brig. Gen. James Barnes's division and Brig. Gen. Roman B. Ayres's division of the Union V Corps were sent to occupy Little Round Top, followed by units of the Union VI Corps later in the evening. This occupation, coupled with the unplanned movement of General Law's Alabama Brigade in that direction, served to fetter the Confederate right to Little Round Top, a hill that originally had no value in relation to Lee's plan, and mostly served as a hindrance—even if captured—to the movement of the rest of Longstreet's corps. It is in this respect that Little Round Top became valuable to the outcome of the battle. Moreover, Federal occupation of Little Round Top served as a prime example of what reinforcements did to enhance the defensibility of Sickles's line.

The other major factor preventing a successful attack along the Emmitsburg Road involved Ewell's movements on the Confederate left. Although not often explored, analysis of events here is essential to understanding why Ewell was so late in identifying an opportunity to commit his corps to a full attack. Four thousand Union troopers of Brig. Gen. David M. Gregg's 2nd Cavalry Division, located east of the town along the Hanover Road, threatened Ewell's rear. This threat represented a peril unique to Ewell's II Corps. Neither Longstreet nor A. P. Hill experienced an enemy force in both their front and rear during July 2. With elements of the Union I, XI, and XII Corps in his front, and with Union cavalry behind and east of his position, Ewell was ordered to look for an opportunity to attack. His circumstances were indeed extraordinary.

The biggest impact the presence of Gregg's cavalry had was that a part of Ewell's corps had to be parceled out along the Hanover Road to hold the Federal force in check. Had Brig. Gen. James A. Walker's brigade of

Virginians, otherwise known as the Stonewall Brigade, not been sent to Brinkerhoff Ridge for this purpose, Maj. Gen. Edward Johnson's division, of which it was a part, might have made a more significant breakthrough at Culp's Hill that evening. Likewise, had Gen. Jubal Early not been forced to weaken his division by sending Brig. Gen. William Smith's brigade to the same area, then East Cemetery Hill might have been attacked with significantly greater numbers. Perhaps with the availability of both brigades, Ewell's demonstration would have become a real attack earlier.

Even with the understanding that Union cavalry threatening Ewell's rear delayed a real attack from the Confederate left, it is essential to recognize that the main attack was to come from Longstreet's corps. It was this attack from the Confederate right that was to be foremost, and from which an "opportunity" for Ewell was to be created, as Lee later stated in his January 1864 report.

Once Ewell's attack began, it was to be a three-pronged strike at the bulwark of the Union line. General Johnson's division was to initiate matters on the Confederate far left, against Culp's Hill. His entry would demand an attack by General Early's division, which was to his right, against East Cemetery Hill. Finally, this approach would invite a strike from General Rodes's division, from the west, toward Cemetery Hill, and thus complete the committal of Ewell's three divisions, in unison from left to right, against the full face of the Union salient. If one pictures Longstreet's attack, which was supported by Maj. Gen. Richard H. Anderson's division of A. P. Hill's corps, joining in cooperation with Ewell, then the overall Confederate plan called for the convergence of Lee's army in the vicinity of Cemetery Hill.

Brig. Gen. Harry T. Hays, commanding the Louisiana Brigade of Early's division, clearly revealed as much in his official report. He noted that while his troops were still struggling with Brig. Gen. Adelbert Ames's division of the XI Corps in order to gain the summit of East Cemetery Hill, he heard the approach of a substantial number of troops to his right, from the direction of West Cemetery Hill. They fired upon his men, but he hesitated to order return fire, even though this unknown force fired three times, because he suspected that these might be friends and not foes. Most interestingly, he specified that he had been "cautioned to expect friends both in front, to the right and to the left—Lieutenant General Longstreet, Major General Rodes and Major General Johnson, respectively having been assigned to these relative positions."[26]

As Hays would later learn, only Early's division actually made it to the top of a part of Cemetery Hill. Without the support and arrival of at least the other two divisions, Hays could not sustain his position, although both Ewell and Early "made every exertion to take [East Cemetery] Hill, which they justly considered as the key to Cemetery Hill, and consequently to our army."[27] Early experienced problems within his own division in terms of supporting Hays's and Col. Isaac Avery's brigades' attacks at East Cemetery Hill. Brig. Gen. John B. Gordon's Georgians hedged to join the fight there, eventually being ordered to stall their brigade at a comfortable distance from the action. To the left of Early's division, Johnson achieved only a foothold at Culp's Hill, while to the right, Rodes's division hesitated along the western slope of Cemetery Hill, believing the Union position there to be too strong. Rodes's inaction seemingly freed up Maj. Gen. Carl Schurz's 1,500 XI Corps troops to shift over and help push Early's division from East Cemetery Hill.

On the Confederate right, Longstreet's oblique attack toward Cemetery Hill ran into a series of obstacles and stoppages. Meade's heavy buttressing of Sickles's line, coupled with the timely arrival of Maj. Gen. John Sedgwick's VI Corps, had supposedly demanded that Longstreet's attack be redirected to meet the crisis at hand. Even so, General Anderson of A. P. Hill's corps attempted to extend his division in the direction of the northern portion of Cemetery Ridge and still maintain the proper course of the Confederate offensive. His efforts were not without merit, as one of his brigades, commanded by Brig. Gen. A. R. Wright, temporarily penetrated that part of Cemetery Ridge, only a couple hundred yards from the southwestern slope of Cemetery Hill.

CHAPTER 7

"The General Plan
Was Unchanged"

Two days of battle had been fought, and for two days the key to unlocking the Union defenses at Gettysburg had eluded General Lee. However, July 3 brought another day and one more opportunity to seize the crucial salient of Cemetery Hill, which protected the major road arteries extending south. It was upon these roads that Meade's Army of the Potomac depended for food, medical supplies, and if need be, access for a retreat south toward Washington.

When Lee found Longstreet on the morning of July 3 near the Round Tops, "Old Pete" had been searching with his scouts for a way, "to move around to the right of Meade's army, and maneuver him into attacking us."[1] Longstreet had either remained convinced or become persuaded that the Union left had to be turned at Little Round Top. The First Corps commander had wanted to make a much broader strategic maneuver around the Union flank as early as July 1. On the morning of July 3, it appeared he was reverting to that line of thought.

When he presented this revised plan to Lee, the commanding general was seemingly less interested in the idea than ever. Longstreet explained it this way: "I was disappointed when he came to me on the morning of the 3d and directed that I should renew the attack against Cemetery Hill. . . . I stated to General Lee that I had been examining the ground over to the right, and was much inclined to think the best thing was to move to the Federal left. 'No,' he said; 'I am going to take them where they are on Cemetery Hill. I want you to take Pickett's Division and make the attack.'"[2]

63

In another rendition of the same conversation, Longstreet recalled that Lee pointed with his fist at Cemetery Hill and replied, "The enemy is there, and I am going to strike him."[3] To which Longstreet retorted, "It is my opinion that no fifteen thousand men ever arrayed for battle can take that position," pointing to Cemetery Hill.[4]

Historians are naturally skeptical of a historical account written a number of years after an event, and therefore some may doubt the accuracy of the details in these two recollections, both recorded more than twenty years after the battle. The further in time one is removed from a historic event, the more likely he is to either embellish the story or create a tale that casts a better light. Some historians may therefore demand that Longstreet's statements quoted above be given less credence than his after-action report, which is chronicled in the *Official Records of the War of the Rebellion*. But in this case, comparing Longstreet's official report with the later accounts reveals remarkable similarities. Consistent on the point of the objective of Pickett's Charge, Longstreet firmly notes that Lee "ordered a column of attack to be formed of Pickett's, Heth's, and part of Pender's divisions, the assault to be made directly at the enemy's main position, the Cemetery Hill."[5]

Ideally, today's students of the battle should be able to cross-reference General Pickett's report with that of Longstreet, to compare their records of the direction and destination of the main attack on July 3. That is not possible, however, since Lee instructed Pickett to destroy his after-action report, presumably because of its inflammatory nature. Nor does the historian have access to other key reports from Confederate officers in the know, such as Brigadier Generals Richard B. Garnett, Lewis A. Armistead, J. L. Kemper, and J. J. Pettigrew, who either died as a result of the charge (the fate of Garnett and Armistead), mortally wounded during the retreat to Virginia (as was Pettigrew), or wounded too badly and recovered too late to write an official report (which prevented Kemper's written testimony).

There is one report other than Longstreet's, written by a participant who belonged to the inner circle of Confederate high command, that points toward Cemetery Hill as the objective of the July 3 attack. That report was written by none other than General Lee himself, and his words provide the necessary key to understanding the Confederate plans for July 3. In his July 31, 1863, official report, Lee stated, "These partial successes determined me to continue the assault the next day."[6] Within the context of these words, one finds the intent for Pickett's Charge, as well as the purpose for all Confederate attacks planned that day. Then, with a hint of admonishment, Lee further proclaimed, "The general plan was unchanged."[7]

"The general plan was unchanged." These five words are the most overlooked and misunderstood of the battle. They are also the most revealing, for Lee's statement both confirms one issue and, at the same time, raises a larger question. First, it verifies that General Lee did indeed operate at the battle of Gettysburg with a general plan in mind. But, perhaps more intriguingly, it also acknowledges that Lee did operate under a general plan on both part of the first day and throughout the second day of the battle. And to suggest that this plan did not change on July 3 is to call into question the standard interpretation of Lee's actions.

The standard interpretation of the battle advances the notion that on the afternoon of July 1, Lee smashed into Union forces west and north of town, with no real aim or purpose, while his opponents cleverly fought a defense in depth. As they did so, they purchased time for the rest of their hard-marching army, which strived to reach Gettysburg and to converge upon the heights south of town. It is traditionally believed that on the second day, Lee set out strictly to attack, bend, and maneuver around the Union flanks. Having failed to turn the flanks on July 2, the Confederate army commander then decided to go straight at the Union center on the third and final day of the battle. This outlook is predicated on the belief that Lee's general plan did change, as he switched from attacking the flanks on July 2 to attacking the center on July 3. But applying this interpretation flies in the face of Lee's statement that "the general plan was unchanged." Within the traditional view, Lee not only changed his plan on the third day, but he did so in radical fashion.

What was Lee trying to accomplish? What is the single connective thread binding together his objectives for the three days? Here are a few clues in retrospect. On the evening of July 1, once Ewell decided he could not attack Cemetery Hill "to advantage," because he could not bring his artillery to bear on it and because his troops were "jaded by twelve hours' marching and fighting," Lee asked Ewell "to draw [his] corps to the right."[8] Presumably, Lee wanted to move him west toward Seminary Ridge, where the slope or ascent to Cemetery Hill was more gradual. Ewell replied that he wanted to remain where he was because he had planned to take possession of a "wooded hill" to his left—Culp's Hill—"on a line with and commanding Cemetery Hill," that "commanded their [the Union] position and made it untenable."[9] Ewell assured Lee that he would take Culp's Hill with

Johnson's division, upon its arrival, and make Cemetery Hill untenable. Meanwhile, Ewell sent a scouting party to Culp's Hill, where most of the men were captured. After this mishap, the corps commander believed the "wooded hill" to be already occupied by the enemy, and with Johnson's arrival after dark, further movements were postponed until the next day.

Lee's plans for July 2 continued where the previous day left off, with Cemetery Hill still the focus. Longstreet was to find the Union left, partially envelop it, and drive it in obliquely toward (not away from) Ewell, the northern portion of Cemetery Ridge, and Cemetery Hill. This attack by the Confederate First Corps was to be the main offensive drive,[10] proceeding up Cemetery Hill by way of its "more gradual slope affording opportunity for success against the Cemetery Hill."[11] During the interim, Ewell was ordered, "as soon as their guns opened, to make a diversion in their [Longstreet's] favor, to be converted into a real attack if an opportunity offered."[12] If Longstreet's movements had met with complete success, then Ewell would have found ample opportunity to join in earlier, thus producing converging Confederate forces at the salient of Cemetery Hill. In effect, the Union left and left center would have been driven in and surrounded at the arc of the Union line. Lee would have successfully brought his outstretched forces together at a "point of impact," as he had done on other battlefields, and would have achieved the victory, north of the Mason-Dixon line, that he so desired. Cemetery Hill would have been the natural point for his left and right wings, under Ewell and Longstreet respectively, to converge and surround.

However, since he had not achieved total success on the first and second day, Lee decided to continue the same "general plan" on the third. He would tidy up unfinished business. Lee believed he could do so because of the "partial successes" up to that point. What partial successes were these? First, the seizure of the Peach Orchard on July 2 provided Lee with the "desired ground" from which to provide artillery support in assaulting "the more elevated heights" of Cemetery Hill. Second, Wright's brigade of Anderson's division had, albeit briefly, broken into the northernmost portion of Cemetery Ridge, where the broader curved hook or salient of the Union line began. Third, the temporary breakthrough of Early's forces at East Cemetery Hill revealed another crack in this same salient. Finally, the lodgment of Brig. Gen. George H. Steuart's brigade, Johnson's division, within Union XII Corps fortifications on Culp's Hill, revealed yet another rupture in this salient arc. All of these "partial successes" shared one achievement:

Each made inroads toward the wide-bending Cemetery Hill salient—the "only hopeful point of attack upon the enemy's entire line."[13] Therefore, on July 3, it was logical and even reasonable to bear down once again on that sector of the Northern army's position. That is exactly what Lee did.

To implement the attack, Lee arranged for Maj. Gen. J. E. B. Stuart's cavalry division—once it arrived at Gettysburg during the afternoon of July 2—to ride east to contest Gregg's cavalry, which had loomed in Ewell's rear. Ewell meanwhile had sent Walker's Stonewall Brigade out along the Hanover Road, where it had grappled with Gregg's cavalry on July 2 at Brinkerhoff Ridge. Consequently, Johnson's division approached Culp's Hill that evening with reduced numbers. It is fair to imagine that with the presence of Walker's brigade, Johnson's division could have forced the brigade of Brig. Gen. George S. "Pap" Greene to abandon its defenses at Culp's Hill on the evening of July 2, before the remainder of the Union XII Corps returned.

Therefore, it stood to reason that if J. E. B. Stuart's Confederate cavalry were to check Gregg's cavalry between the York and Hanover Roads, then Walker's brigade could be released to come up to the previously exploited area of lower Culp's Hill. Lee did not stop there, however. Both Brig. Gen. Junius Daniel's and Col. E. A. O'Neil's brigades, from Rodes's division, along with Brig. Gen. William "Extra Billy" Smith's brigade, from Early's division, were shifted to Culp's Hill during the early hours of July 3. With the arrival and placement of Stuart's cavalry in Ewell's rear, holding Union cavalry in check on the Confederate far left, it became possible to rectify the coordination problems of July 2 with a renewed attack on July 3.

CHAPTER 8

Day Three:
Pickett's Charge

On the morning of July 3, according to the traditional version of the battle, Lee still does not have an objective, but rather is making up his battle plan as he goes along, leaving his corps commanders unaware of his next move as he fails to hold a council of war. The most credit Lee is given for having a plan is that he sought to turn both flanks of the army on July 3, but gave up on this idea when Little Round Top was deemed too strong to turn. In this version of events, Longstreet's idea of a broader maneuver around the Union left makes sense because, after all, Lee did not have a plan. It is at this point that Ewell's role on July 3 becomes an unrelated sideshow for believers of the affirmed version of events, as Longstreet is released from cooperating with him. The correlation between Confederate reinforcements massing against the Culp's Hill side of the Cemetery Hill salient and Lee's insistence that Pickett do the same from the other side becomes irrelevant.

As Ewell was busy overseeing the buildup of Confederate reinforcements at Culp's Hill, Lee seemingly expected Longstreet to be doing the same opposite the western face of Cemetery Hill. It has not been popular in recent years to suggest that Lee gave Longstreet orders for a "sunrise attack," but it is hard not to question why General Pickett was not summoned up to the field the previous evening. His division was only three to four miles west of Seminary Ridge when it halted during the evening of July 2. If "the general plan was unchanged," why did Longstreet not order Pickett's division onto the field? Lee's own words raise this question when he states that

Alfred R. Waud completed "Longstreet's Assault" for Harper's Weekly, *August 8, 1863. Based on eyewitness sketches, it was one of the first images of the charge to appear in the Northern press. Here, Pickett is trying to take Hancock's men by flank and drive them to Pettigrew's front. Note the waves of attack coming at the oblique. From Waud's perspective, the nearly ninety-degree angle that Pickett's division formed with the Emmitsburg Road is clearly visible. By the time Pickett's division had crossed this road, they were more perpendicular to Pettigrew's division than a continuation of the same line. Pickett's division also can be seen marching "up the Emmitsburg Road," carrying out the unfinished work of Hood's division from the day before.* GETTYSBURG NATIONAL MILITARY PARK ARCHIVES; PHOTOGRAPH BY ALAN WYCHECK

"Longstreet, reinforced by Pickett's three brigades, which arrived near the battlefield during the afternoon of the 2nd, was ordered to attack the next morning, and General Ewell was directed to assail the enemy's right at the same time."[1]

How could Lee have stated his objectives any more clearly? Ewell and Longstreet were to try to coordinate their attacks once again. If Longstreet had been ordered to "attack the next morning," we must assume that Lee expected Pickett to be at Seminary Ridge, ready to attack, much earlier than he was. This was clarified by Col. E. P. Alexander: "During the evening [of July 2] I found my way to General Longstreet's bivouac, a little ways in the rear. . . . I was told that we would renew the attack early in the morning. That Pickett's division would arrive and would assault the enemy's line. My impression is the exact point for it was not designated, but I was told it would be to our left of the Peach Orchard." This information, given to Alexander by Longstreet's staff, proved to be reliable. A few hours later, Pickett's division formed and attacked to the left of Alexander's artillery position, which began at the orchard.[2] So if Longstreet knew that Lee wanted to renew the attack against Cemetery Hill and that Pickett's division had to be placed on the left of his corps to achieve this, then one might expect that he would be ready. And in fact, Lee stated, "General Longstreet's dispositions were not completed as early as was expected."[3] Moreover, Lee added that Johnson's efforts at Culp's Hill were defeated on the morning of July 3 because, "the projected attack on the enemy's left not having been made, he [Meade] was enabled to hold his right with a force largely superior to that of General Johnson, and finally to threaten his flank and rear, rendering it necessary for him to retire to his original position about 1 P.M."[4]

Plainly, Lee was suggesting that Johnson's Culp's Hill failures against the Union XII Corps during the morning of July 3 were directly related to the absence of an attack by Longstreet at the same time, on the western side of the salient. Lee understood that coordinated pressure on both sides of the Union line largely prevented Meade from shifting troops. The scope of the attack that Lee visualized for July 3 was even larger than that. When Lee alluded to "the projected attack on the enemy's left," he was not merely referring to Pickett's division of Longstreet's corps making the assault from that sector. Lee conceived that Hood's and McLaws's divisions of Longstreet's corps were also to advance forward with Pickett. According to Lee, Hood and McLaws had to move forward because "the general plan of attack was unchanged, excepting that one division and two brigades of [A. P.] Hill's corps were ordered to support Longstreet."[5]

Hood's and McLaws's divisions were to at least pin down the Union left while Pickett's division struck the more northern portions of Cemetery Ridge, overrunning the Union defenses perhaps where Wright's Georgia Brigade had penetrated less than twenty-four hours earlier. In doing so, they were to drive Hancock's Union II Corps, bolstered by the remnants of the I Corps, back toward Cemetery Hill. To further support this move, the divisions of Pettigrew and Trimble of A. P. Hill's corps were expected to attack the southwestern portion of Cemetery Hill, on Pickett's left. Meanwhile, the brigades of Wilcox and Lang, also from Hill's corps, were to closely follow and protect Pickett's right.

The Pickett-Pettigrew-Trimble charge was not meant to be a solo mission. To explain the charge in this one-dimensional fashion, leaving out the brigades of Wilcox and Lang and divisions of Hood and McLaws, on Pickett's right, while ignoring the efforts of Johnson's, Early's, and Rodes's divisions, and Stuart's cavalry on the Confederate left, is simply inaccurate. Conversely, to present the fight of Johnson's division at Culp's Hill as a sideshow, not directly related to the events between Seminary and Cemetery Ridges, is to miss the whole purpose behind Lee's plans for that momentous day. It is pointless to investigate Lee's reasons for deciding to make Pickett's Charge if one does not address the depth, breadth, and scope of the planned attack, which was intended to cover the entire Union battle line. Because Pickett was not able to coordinate with Johnson, and because Longstreet elected not to send in Hood and McLaws, does that justify treating Pickett's Charge as a separate action? Or should it be that, as Jubal Early later stated, "in order to judge the propriety of making the attacks on the 2d and 3d, we should consider the circumstances and conditions under which

---

OPPOSITE PAGE: This map shows what Lee ideally visualized on July 3. On July 2, Lee's line had become overextended as a result of the distraction of Little Round Top on Longstreet's far right. On July 3, Lee wanted to converge his army by having Longstreet's corps, bolstered by Pickett's division on the left, join Hood and McLaws, who were to cut more north above Little Round Top. Longstreet later said that the goal was to drive the Union left in upon its center, toward the town. Lee wanted his infantry lines to become increasingly stronger as they condensed and came to a point of impact at Cemetery Hill. Had the Union line not beaten back the assault, even as it actually occurred, with Pickett's men bearing the weight of the attack, the effects could have proven disastrous. If Lee had taken Cemetery Hill, he would have cut the Union off from both the town and the head of the road juncture, separating the Union army and forcing its extremities to retreat down Taneytown Road and the Baltimore Pike. Stuart's cavalry was situated within easy reach of the Baltimore Pike to harass the miles of Union wheeled vehicles sure to pass that way during a retreat.

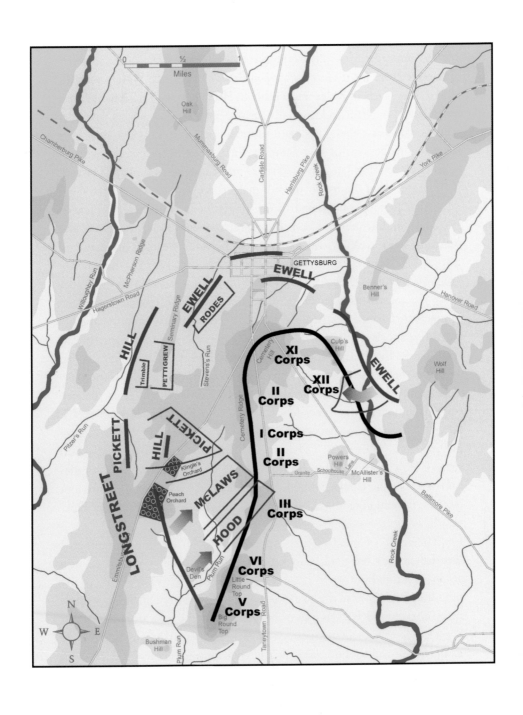

those attacks were ordered, and not merely their failure from other circumstances and conditions beyond the control of the Commander-in-Chief."[6]

In Longstreet's favor, the fact that two brigades of Union cavalry, belonging to Brig. Gen. Elon J. Farnsworth and Brig. Gen. Wesley Merritt,
posted near Warfield Ridge and Bushman Hill, on Hood's right flank, must
have made Longstreet additionally nervous of an attack on his rear. It is
quite possible that he did not want to invite such a Union move by risking
a forward movement of Hood and McLaws. Even so, there seems to be
scant evidence that Lee canceled that part of the "general plan." Lee's report, written after the battle, did not make this exemption.

Other factors contributed to the unplanned solo attack by Pickett,
Pettigrew, and Trimble. When the charge moved forward, its flanks and
rear were to be covered and supported by horse-drawn light artillery. Lee
recorded, "The batteries were directed to be pushed forward as the infantry
progressed, protect their flanks, and support their attacks closely."[7] But because the massed cannonade, which came before the charge, continued
significantly beyond its scheduled time of twenty to thirty minutes, and because Capt. J. B. Richardson's 2nd Company of Louisiana howitzers was
temporarily lost during the bombardment, Pickett's Charge proceeded
across the fields with its flanks bare and exposed. Lee reported it this way:
"Our own [batteries] having nearly exhausted their ammunition in the pro-
tracted cannonade that preceded the advance of the infantry, were unable
to reply, or render the necessary support to the attacking party."[8] Consequently, Maj. Thomas W. Osborn's XI Corps batteries on Cemetery Hill
raked Col. J. M. Brockenbrough's and Brig. Gen. Joseph R. Davis's brigades
on the left of the charge, while Lt. Col. Freeman McGilvery's twenty-four
or more Federal guns shredded Kemper's brigade on the far right of Pickett's line.

The results of failed artillery support during the assault were profound.
On the charge's left flank, Brockenbrough's Virginia Brigade halted in a
swale, about midway across the field. No doubt the direct approach of the
8th Ohio Infantry from the southwest slope of Cemetery Hill, firing a volley
into Brockenbrough's Virginia troops, contributed to the stopping of this
brigade. However, the helplessness of A. P. Hill's artillery along Seminary
Ridge to respond to the Cemetery Hill guns during the charge jeopardized
any real infantry effectiveness there. "Massed as were the enemy's batteries
on the Cemetery Hill, fronting our left, and commanding as was their position," noted Confederate artillery chief Brig. Gen. William N. Pendleton,

"our artillery, admirably served as it was, operated there under serious disadvantage and with considerable loss."[9] The ultimate result of Confederate artillery ineffectiveness in that sector was that the left of the charge was flanked and enfiladed by part of Brig. Gen. Alexander Hays's 3rd Division, Union II Corps.

Without artillery support on Pickett's right, McGilvery's Union artillery, which was located in the vicinity of where the Pennsylvania Memorial now stands, had an uncontested and clean field of fire into the line there. The great advantage of the position McGilvery possessed from which to enfilade Kemper's line is hard to visualize today because of the dense growth of trees there, which in 1863 consisted of perhaps only eighteen trees.[10] Adding to Kemper's misery, Lt. Benjamin F. Rittenhouse's battery of Federal guns on Little Round Top was even able to lob a few solid shots and shells from above. Rittenhouse's guns were perhaps able to turn their attention to the task of harassing Pickett's right flank because McLaws's and Hood's divisions were not ordered forward.

The collapse of Pickett's right flank has contributed to the misunderstanding of the event by blurring the purpose, direction, and design of the whole charge. Understanding this fact is absolutely crucial to grasping Lee's intentions throughout the battle. Union enfilading fire damaged Pickett's flank so seriously that the emphasis of the charge lost its shape, leaving the modern historian with a false understanding of the assault's true intent. With the shattering of Pickett's right flank, and with the charge's designed tendency to dress left toward Pettigrew's division, the Confederate attackers progressively crowded together in front of the now canonized "copse of trees." Jumbled and bunched together there, with both Confederate flanks having collapsed, Pickett's men, along with several regiments of Pettigrew's division, appeared to be focusing solely on that position. Again, their final destination reflected their failed state rather than Lee's original plan.

What, then, was the true tactical intent of the charge? Simply, it was to be a grand general movement diagonally toward Cemetery Hill, with an intent to drive the Cemetery Ridge defenders there. Had the flanks remained protected, the intent and direction of the charge would have been apparent. Most evident would have been that the aiming point was Ziegler's Grove, and not the copse of trees.[11]

Additional detail on the deployment of Longstreet's troops, just prior to the assault, is also helpful in understanding the true intent of the charge. To this point, Pickett's three brigades, which were deployed in swales east

The heavy woods of Codori thicket, photographed in January 2000. In July 1863 this area consisted of only a few isolated trees. These trees are gradually being thinned out as part of the Gettysburg National Military Park's General Management Plan. For decades, the woods have prevented a view of the position of McGilvery's Union artillery battalion, which fired from a position just on the other side into the right wing of Pickett's division, which passed from right to left in front of these postwar trees. The Emmitsburg Road can be seen in front of the woods.
PHOTOGRAPH BY LISA HARMAN

A more recent view of Codori thicket, taken in January 2003, showing the progress of the tree-thinning plan. Many of the trees seen in the photo above were removed in 2002, allowing for glimpses of McGilvery's artillery position during the months when the leaves are absent. PHOTOGRAPH BY LISA HARMAN of Seminary Ridge, were posted to the right and considerably in front of Pettigrew and Trimble. This fact is often obscured by the popular myth that Pickett's division started its attack from the woods. Actually, the two lead brigades of Garnett and Kemper, or two-thirds of Pickett's division, were deployed throughout the cannonade in a swale at least 200 yards in advance of the woods. Moreover, the brigades of Wilcox and Lang, which were to support Pickett's right flank, were deployed as far forward as the Emmitsburg Road ridge. Only Brig. Gen. Lewis A. Armistead's brigade, which trailed in rear of the charge most of the way, was positioned near a protrusion of trees known as the "point of woods," closer to Seminary Ridge. Even so, his men were depending on the cover of a swale there rather than the woods, which at best would have cast a shadow on Armistead's double-ranked lines. Other than shade, the woods would have offered only danger that day, as they were a noticeable landmark toward which Union artillery could direct their fire.

So then, most of Pickett's division was posted out of view of Union artillery, in low swales, considerably east of Seminary Ridge. Even the rear brigade under Armistead would have been roughly 100 yards in front of the peak of the ridge as he sought to move beyond the "point of woods." Meanwhile, Pettigrew's and Trimble's brigades, to the left of Pickett, were positioned in a swale west of and behind Seminary Ridge, which afforded them cover. Consequently, when the infantry assault began at about 3 P.M., these two supporting divisions of A. P. Hill's corps would have appeared to lag behind at first, but that was by design. In actuality, they would follow a more direct route to Cemetery Ridge than Pickett, covering less ground, which eventually compensated for their precannonade deployment behind Seminary Ridge.

There are so many repeated falsehoods about Pickett's Charge that it is hard to address them all here. One of them maintains that Pickett's division made its oblique forty-five-degree turn to the left during the assault as a last-minute reaction to the geography, which was pulling their course to the right. Another commonly held belief states that this oblique maneuver was included in the charge in order to bring converging fire, along with Pettigrew's men, down on the small angle at the stone wall near the "copse of trees," which in July 1863 would be better described as the "group of bushes."[12] In reality, this move was instituted that day for neither of these reasons. Rather, it was part of a predetermined plan by General Lee, which held a deeper purpose.

The purpose of the oblique maneuver on the third day of the battle was relative to its purpose the day before. The oblique order of battle was one of Lee's favorite tactics, as "it involved . . . rolling up his [enemy's] flank as successive parts of his own line made contact."[13] But even more important than "successive parts" coming into play, which an echelon at-tack also offered, was the diagonal approach taken toward the side of a de-fender. If brought in at a slant, the attacker would present indirect fire while avoiding straightforward, linear fire. It was for these advantages that the oblique order of battle proved to be Lee's choice of action again on the third day.

Apparently, when Lee recorded in his report that "the general plan was unchanged," he was also referring to the specific tactical order that sent his men on their oblique advance. Soon after Pickett's division emerged from its swales, making an abrupt left turn just before it crossed the Emmitsburg Road (with its left connected to the road and its right extended southeast,

STANNARD'S BRIGADE OPENING ON PICKETT'S DIVISION.

"Stannard's Brigade Opening On Pickett's Division, Gettysburg, July 3d, 1863." Commissioned by Col. John Bachelder and completed just four years after the battle, this portrayal further reinforces the distinct oblique course to which Pickett's troops adhered, even to the point of presenting their flank to an enfilade fire. GETTYSBURG NATIONAL MILITARY PARK ARCHIVES

forming a right angle), the attack must have borne an uncanny resemblance to Hood's "attack up the Emmitsburg Road" the day before. In its very essence, Pickett's oblique attack represented the natural progression and continuation of Hood's attack from the previous day. Even Pettigrew's positional relationship and proximity to Pickett, at the point of the oblique, should have resembled McLaws's to Hood nearly twenty-four hours earlier. From an artillery standpoint, the essential nature of the Peach Orchard as "desired ground" for enfilading Cemetery Ridge, in support of such an attack, had not changed.

Other comparisons between Longstreet's attack on July 2 and July 3 can be made. One such comparison shows that if Pickett's right wing had been successful in penetrating the Cemetery Ridge line, to begin the process of rolling up the Federal position toward Cemetery Hill, in all probability that point would have been where Lee perceived that the Federal army's left flank would have ended when he devised plans for July 2. There were only two differences from the previous day's assault. First, A. P. Hill supplied Heth's and Pender's divisions to support the plan, efforts led by Pettigrew and Trimble, respectively. Second, the thrust of the oblique order of battle was moved closer to the mark of Cemetery Hill.

As the Confederate infantry moved forward, with Pickett's division turning forty-five degrees left and continually dressing left to connect with a trailing Pettigrew, the charge must have resembled a mile-wide crescent, gradually conforming to the outer circumference of Cemetery Hill. Maj. Gen. Winfield Scott Hancock, who commanded the Union center that day, later testified before Congress, "When the columns of the enemy appeared it looked as if they were going to attack the centre of our [Hancock's] line, but after marching straight out a little distance they seemed to incline a little to their left, as if their object was to march through my command and seize Cemetery hill, which I have no doubt was their intention."[14] Col. Edward Porter Alexander, entrusted with the command of the artillery supporting Pickett's division, concurred that Confederate movements needed to move left as they sought to conform to Cemetery Hill. He noted, "Early in the morning General Lee came around, and I was then told that we were to assault Cemetery Hill, which lay rather to our left."[15]

Although E. P. Alexander had "second thoughts" in later years as to the purpose and ultimate destination of the charge, the preponderance of the evidence strongly favors the opinion that he knew as well as Longstreet, Hancock, and Pickett that Cemetery Hill was Lee's final goal. Not only is this evident in his earlier writings, but it is also actually clear in all of his writings except *Military Memoirs of a Confederate,* which appeared much later, in 1907. Alexander also revealed in at least one earlier writing that he exactly understood the difference between Cemetery Ridge and Cemetery Hill.

Starting with his earliest writings and working forward, it is clear that Alexander persisted in the opinion that Cemetery Hill was Lee's final objective. On August 10, 1863, Alexander reported to Col. Gilbert Moxley Sorrel, "I wrote to General Pickett that unless he advanced immediately the artillery . . . would give him but little support . . . the enemy was still firing vigorously and at least eighteen guns were firing directly from the point (the cemetery) he was to charge."[16] Similarly, in a letter to archivist and historian John B. Bachelder dated May 3, 1876, Alexander stated, "[I] had orders to prepare for an assault on Cemetery Hill somewhere about 8 a.m. on the 3rd as I recollect perhaps earlier."[17] Slightly more than a year later, he documented to Rev. J. William Jones, "Before daylight on the morning of the 3d I received orders to post the artillery for an assault upon the enemy's position, and later I learned that it was to be led by Pickett's Division and directed on Cemetery Hill."[18] Four years later, he recalled with comparable detail, "Before daylight on the morning of the 3rd I received orders to post the artillery for an assault on the enemy's position, and later learned it was to be led by Pickett's Division and directed on Cemetery Hill."[19] He added, ". . . as I had heard it said that morning that Gen. Lee had ordered 'every brigade in the Army to charge Cemetery Hill,' and it was certain that the question of supports had had [Lee's] careful attention."[20]

Three to six years later, sometime between 1884 and 1887, Alexander submitted an account of Pickett's Charge to *Battles and Leaders.* More so than in any other account, he made it clear that he understood the difference between Cemetery Hill and Ridge:

> Early in the morning General Lee came around, and I was then told that we were to assault Cemetery Hill, which lay rather to our left . . . we had seventy-five guns in what was virtually one battery, so disposed as to fire on Cemetery Hill and the batteries south of it, which would have a fire on our advancing infantry. . . . It had been arranged that when the infantry column was ready, General Longstreet

should order two guns fired by the Washington Artillery. On that signal all our guns were to open on Cemetery Hill and the ridge extending toward Round Top.[21]

From the late 1880s to 1890s, Alexander again related in his personal memoirs, "I had heard a sort of camp rumor, that morning, that Gen. Lee had said he intended to march every man he had upon that cemetery hill that day."[22] In the same text, as Alexander described the final moments of the precharge cannonade, he noted: "At least 18 guns are still firing from the cemetery itself. This was the point of direction of the storming column. The brigade of direction was [Col. B. D.] Fry's, the right brigade of Pettigrew's line. It was to march on the cemetery & the rest of the line was to dress upon it."[23]

It is only in his last written account that Alexander expressed doubts that Cemetery Hill was the final goal. Forty-four years after the charge, he voiced his first uncertainty, stating that "comparatively the weakest portion of their line was Cemetery Hill, and the point of greatest interest in connection with this battle is the story of our entire failure to recognize this fact."[24] At this point in his life, Alexander had seemingly fallen in love with his idea that Cemetery Hill should have been assaulted from the southern edge of the town, where he believed Confederate guns could have better enfiladed XI Corps guns on Cemetery Hill, and where charging Confederates could have better avoided the enfilade of Union guns. The side effect of his theory, upon which he never elaborated, was that a Confederate attack made directly from the town would have drawn Union artillery fire onto the town. In this case, Lee would have betrayed his own orders regarding the destruction of civilian property. Maybe that is why Lee avoided launching his main attack on July 3 from that position.

Perhaps Alexander's late-life confusion about the destination of Pickett's Charge resulted from the rise in prominence of John B. Bachelder's "copse of trees" theory, as it related to the battle's July 3 story line. The affirmed version was becoming established by 1907, with the copse of trees becoming the focal point of the Confederacy's high water mark. Meanwhile, Cemetery Hill as a tactical position was already becoming a secondary theme. After the copse of trees concept was introduced to Alexander as a central part of the story—perhaps by the engineer Lt. Col. E. B. Cope during Alexander's visit to the Gettysburg battlefield on May 30, 1894—he must have become unsure of where the assaulting column

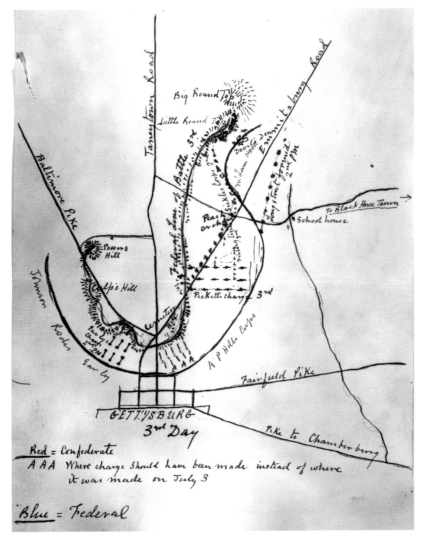

Sketched by Col. Edward Porter Alexander, c. 1889, this map of the battlefield illustrates the distance of Lee's greatly extended exterior line versus the more compact, interior line occupied by Meade. By the time he made this sketch, Alexander had begun to believe that Cemetery Hill should have been assaulted from the direction of the town, which might have avoided direct fire from Union XI Corps guns, and enabled an enfilade of those guns by Confederate attackers.

was headed on July 3. His confusion would have been increased by the absence of Ziegler's Grove, which had been felled more than a decade earlier.[25] For thirty-one years, he had understood the cemetery itself or Cemetery Hill to be the primary Confederate objective, but then Cope probably explained it much differently. And, as have countless others over the years, Alexander must have contemplated why and how merely breaking the Union center there would have achieved victory.

In 1907, under the fog of a new uncertainty, he wrote, "A clump of trees in the enemy's line was pointed out to me as the proposed point of the attack, which I was incorrectly told was the cemetery of the town."[26] Again, because Alexander did not mention the copse of trees in his earlier accounts, it is likely that they were introduced to him as important only later in his life, and only after 1888—he visited just six years later—when they were deemed important.

CHAPTER 9

A Reassessment of Pickett's Charge

For the serious student of the battle, there is one conspicuous obstacle to accepting the idea that Pickett, Pettigrew, and Trimble were to march on and assault Cemetery Hill. According to the battle's accepted written history, the copse of trees was the target of the assault, which places the final objective of the attack along Cemetery Ridge. Accompanying this idea is the notion that Pettigrew swerved to the right toward the copse, as Pickett veered left to the same point, in an attempt to bring converging fire on a mini angle at the small stone wall along Cemetery Ridge.

Concluding that the traditionally recognized copse of trees marked the position of Confederate attack raises some puzzling questions. Their answers illuminate some serious shortcomings in the traditionally accepted view of the incident. Were Pickett's men and many of Pettigrew's men stopped in that vicinity? Yes. Were the copse of trees and the Union troops who defended that area within the path of Pickett's attack? Absolutely. Confederate attackers were certainly not trying to avoid Brig. Gen. Alexander S. Webb's brigade of Gibbon's 2nd Division. Their intention was to attack him in full force. Webb's four Pennsylvania regiments and the copse of trees were directly in the path of attack. With this in mind, the more pertinent question becomes whether Webb's position, as marked by the copse of trees, was intended to be the focal point and/or ultimate goal of the charge. The answer is that it was probably not.

The two major players in the event—Longstreet, who was commander of the charge, and Hancock, who commanded the Union defense—clearly

85

BATTLE OF GETTYSBURG, FRIDAY, JULY 3d, 1863.
FROM A SKETCH BY EDWIN FORBES

This engraving of an Edwin Forbes's sketch, "Battle of Gettysburg, Friday July 3d, 1863," again conspicuously features Ziegler's Grove to the left and the woods at Evergreen Cemetery to the right and beyond. The entire charge is portrayed as conforming to the main Cemetery Hill. At the present time, this view from Seminary Ridge is impossible: The Cyclorama Center alone blocks most of this picture. GETTYSBURG NATIONAL MILITARY PARK ARCHIVES

did not place the charge's final goal at the traditionally recognized spot. On the contrary, in every account Longstreet wrote, he stated that he was ordered to attack the main position of Cemetery Hill, also making it clear that he understood the difference between Cemetery Ridge and Cemetery Hill. Likewise, Hancock unequivocally testified that the Confederate objective was "to march through my command and seize Cemetery Hill, which I have no doubt was their intention."[1] Lee's own military secretary, A. L. Long, who was with Lee on July 3 and who later wrote the general's memoirs, assessed:

> There was, however, a weak point . . . where the [cemetery] ridge, sloping westward, formed the depression through which the Emmitsburg road passes. Perceiving that by forcing the Federal lines at that point [Emmitsburg Road] and turning [obliquing] toward Cemetery Hill the right [Hays's 3rd Division] would be taken in flank

[with the oblique maneuver] and the remainder would be
neutralized as its fire would be as destructive to friend as
foe. . . . General Lee determined to attack at that point,
and the execution of it was assigned to Longstreet.[2]

Further reinforcing the matter, General Pickett, whose report was destroyed, did leave extracts that also pointed to the same goal.[3] In one such
excerpt, he noted, "Early in the morning I was assured by E. P. Alexander
that General Lee had ordered every brigade in his [Lee's] command to
charge Cemetery Hill, so I had no fear of not being supported."[4]

Confederate war correspondent Peter Wellington Alexander, who was
an eyewitness and privy to information from the Confederate high command, editorialized on July 4, 1863, that "Pickett's Virginia division, Longstreet's corps, which had only arrived the night before, was ordered to
assault Cemetery Hill, which was considered the key to the enemy's whole
position . . . and he succeeded in wresting a portion of the hill." From Mar-
tinsburg, Virginia, on July 14, 1863, he reiterated, "On the 3rd, Pickett's division of Longstreet's corps (which had come up the evening before),
supported by a portion of Hill's corps, was ordered to assault Cemetery Hill
near the center, believed to be the key to the position of the enemy."[5]

Longstreet, Hancock, Pickett, A. L. Long, Peter W. Alexander, and
even E. P. Alexander all verified that Cemetery Hill was Lee's objective for
July 3. These corroborating claims from men of such importance should au-
tomatically call into question the validity of the affirmed position that the
copse of trees was the central terrain feature. The thinking historian con-
siders, "Should not Pickett, Pettigrew, and Trimble have been aiming for
some landmark closer to Cemetery Hill?" It should be obvious that the affirmed version of the battle asserts a point of focus for Longstreet's assault
that does not precisely mark the "main position, the Cemetery Hill,"
which Longstreet claimed as his objective in his own after-action report.[6]
In reality, this aiming point was of no real strategic value to Lee's army.
Taking that low ridge alone, which was dominated by Cemetery Hill just
to the north, achieved no greater purpose. The ridge alone was a dead end.

Kathy Georg Harrison was the first modern historian to investigate the
possibility that the traditionally recognized position at the copse of trees
might not have been the goal of the charge. In her 1981 work, "Common
Pride and Fame," Harrison, a senior historian at Gettysburg National Military Park, asks, "The Objective Point of the Assault: The Clump of Trees

or Ziegler's Grove?"[7] She argues that the "clump" or "copse of trees" became the point of direction for the charge only during the postwar memorialization period, and that it was the central creation of one individual: John B. Bachelder, an influential director of the Gettysburg Battlefield Memorial Association. Harrison traces the origin of Bachelder's invention back to a casual conversation he had with Walter Harrison, a former adjutant and inspector in Pickett's division, in the postwar years at Gettysburg. She uncovered a revealing correspondence in which Bachelder reminisces:

> I invited Colonel Harrison to visit the battlefield with me, and we spent several hours under the shade cast by the copse of trees, when he explained to me what an important feature that copse of trees was at the time of the battle, and how it had been a landmark towards which Longstreet's assault of July 3d 1863 had been directed. Impressed with its importance, I remarked, "Why Colonel, as the battle of Gettysburg was the crowning event, of this campaign, this copse of trees must have been the high water mark of the rebellion." To which he assented, and from that time on, I felt a reverence for those trees. . . . The thought of naming the copse of trees the "High Water Mark of the Rebellion," and the idea of perpetuating its memory by a monument, was mine.[8]

Kathy Harrison builds upon this revelation and shows how Bachelder nurtured and preserved most of those trees, pushing for their enshrinement by encircling them with an iron fence and proposing a resolution at the September 25, 1888, meeting of the Executive Committee "that a bronze tablet be prepared, indicating and setting forth the movements of troops at the copse of trees on Hancock Avenue, July 3d 1863, which passed unanimously."[9]

Bachelder's unilateral memorialization of the copse led to a rush of Union veterans to place their monuments in that area. The concept of a "high water mark" of the Confederacy was literally landscaped into existence. In fact, so much interest was drawn to the location that some units placed their monuments there in error, and a few were even removed. In their zeal to be associated with the spot Bachelder had designated as where the Confederacy lost the war, every Union regiment—even those that did not fight near the copse—wanted to stake their claim in stone as close to the trees as possible.

Along with this development arose the propensity of veterans to recognize the importance of those trees in their writings, which largely came after Bachelder had memorialized them. According to Harrison, "Those accounts which referred to the growth as the 'copse of trees' were primarily written in the late 1880s–1900s, after Bachelder's idea germinated and spawned a cast-iron fence and bronze tablet. The uniformity of opinion concerning this copse of trees notion that this landmark was the objective point of Pickett's Charge was not commonly accepted or communicated until after 1886." Harrison continues, "By the time the War Department took over administration of the Gettysburg Battlefield in 1895, the story that the clump of trees was the objective of Lee's attack on July 3 was accepted as fact and preached by the Park Commission as doctrine."[10]

Harrison argues that Ziegler's Grove, not the copse of trees, was the more logical focal point of the attack. To support her theory, Harrison offers the writing of the Comte de Paris, a French aristocrat, historian, and author of *History of the Civil War in America*. His comments, published in 1883—five years before Bachelder's efforts to distinguish the copse of trees—state that "between seven and eight o'clock in the morning [of July 3], when the conflict had been progressing along the left [Culp's Hill] for at least four hours, [Lee] is still occupied in assigning places to the troops that are to make an attack upon Ziegler's Grove."[11] Reiterating the point, the comte also remarked, "In the prolongation at the south-west of the hillock properly called Cemetery Hill stands the plateau designated by Lee as the objective point of the attack, which we shall call Ziegler's Grove, from the name of a small wood which descends the slope opposite Gettysburg."[12]

In 1919, George Thornton Fleming, editor of the biography *Life and Letters of Brigadier General Alexander Hays*, set out to express the opinion of Hays and the veterans of his 3rd Division, Union II Corps, regarding the focal point of Pickett's Charge. Since it was Hays's men who defended the area in front of Ziegler's Grove, they naturally would have had a biased opinion concerning the importance of their position, but no more so than that of Webb's men, who defended the copse of trees. Hays's biography states:

> The assault at the time seemed to have culminated in the
> Third Division front, and from the number of prisoners

and flags taken by the Third Division we knew it did. This brings us to the question of direction. We of Hays's Division have always contended that Ziegler's Grove was to be the striking point of the enemy. It was a better point, both of vantage and, from the view of a landmark, more prominent than the copse of trees on Webb's left, then mere saplings and on a low ground. Now, in the growth of half a century naturally prominent, but then inconspicuous in comparison with the heavy timber of Ziegler's Grove. . . . Today the stately timber of Ziegler's Grove and its commanding position appeal to an observer on Lee's line on what is now known as West Confederate Avenue. On that line one naturally searches for the copse of trees to find it. The grove [Ziegler's] and its tall oaks, stately and commanding, impress one as he surveys the position from the Confederate position in its front, and only the lower portion of the grove is visible, that part of the slope east of the Bryan house. At the time of the battle the trees here were thick and gave the appearance of a clump. They were sufficiently thick to afford a distinctive landmark and a point of direction that would loom up in more prominence than the thin saplings in the copse.[13]

Kathy Harrison offers one further piece of evidence to support her claim that Ziegler's Grove was the point of direction for Pickett, Pettigrew, and Trimble. In a letter dated November 29, 1909, Col. Clinton D. MacDougall, former commander of the 111th New York Infantry, 3rd Division, claimed: "The main point of attack was Ziegler's Grove, just to our right and rear, and near the Bryan house. The crowding of the attacking party was from their right to left, showing conclusively that Ziegler's Grove was the point aimed at and not the small clump of undergrowth on the much lower ground on our left, which has been so much written about as the 'high water mark of the Rebellion.'"[14]

Colonel MacDougall's account is especially useful to understanding the point of direction for the charge, because it contains a crucial clue to a related line of argument: the phrase "the crowding of the attacking party was from their right to left." Students of the battle are aware that officers of

Pickett's division probably agreed at the brigade level, moments before the charge, to dress left to connect with Pettigrew. Therefore, Pickett's aiming point became linked to the movements of Pettigrew, who seems to have moved in a more straightforward direction toward Ziegler's Grove. In other words, the evidence strongly suggests that Pettigrew's men did not make a right oblique back in the direction of the copse of trees, which they would have had to do if their objective was to merely break the Union line at the area now designated as an important salient.[15] Mapmakers have for years mistakenly drawn Pettigrew's route as one of a right oblique. It is tempting for the cartographer to sketch or trace Pettigrew and Trimble on a swerve right course, but such a movement is largely unsupported by existing evidence. Pettigrew's division would have dressed right to assure a connection with Pickett, but that would have been the extent of it.

Even if one accepts that Colonel Fry's brigade, which formed the right flank of Pettigrew's division, charted out the direction of march, it is clear that Fry also missed reaching the copse of trees.[16] In a larger sense, the majority of Pettigrew's division, to Fry's left, stood considerably closer to Ziegler's Grove than to the other trees, and undeniably most of Trimble's division, eventually on their left, charged directly toward Ziegler's Grove. Indeed, the majority of Trimble's men were on a course far removed from the copse of trees. Even though the left of Pettigrew's and Trimble's lines was flanked and pressured to move right to some degree, still none of those men actually attacked in front of the copse of trees. Instead, "They made their assault in front of Hays's and Gibbon's Divisions, Second Corps, in the vicinity of Ziegler's Grove."[17] Those two whole Confederate divisions remained north of the copse of trees and somewhat isolated from them.

General Hancock's observations allude to the fact that pressure against Trimble's and Pettigrew's left was a factor. Hancock seemed to recognize that Pettigrew's troops did not set out with the mission of bearing to their right, but that some of them did so only as a reaction to the crisis of the collapse of their left. They were supposed to dress right to assure a connection with Pickett, but that maneuver is far different from the one that actually took place in the assault's final stages. Hancock remembered it this way: "Those of the enemy's troops who did not fall into disorder in front of the Third [Hays's] Division were moved to the right, and reinforced the line [Pickett's] attacking Gibbon's [2nd] Division."[18] Lt. Col. John T. Jones of the 26th North Carolina, Pettigrew's division, confirmed Hancock's viewpoint when he somewhat reluctantly disclosed, "Here candor compels me to admit that one of the brigades of our division had given way, the enemy had seized upon the gap, and now poured a galling fire into our left, which compelled the troops to give way in succession to the right."[19]

Lt. L. E. Bicknell, of the 1st Massachusetts Sharpshooters, offered his perspective on how pressure against the Confederate left affected the outcome of the charge. As one of the participants responsible for applying that pressure, he recalled:

> The last [Confederate] division of the charging column . . . crossing the Emmitsburg road, moving direct for Ziegler's Grove . . . this fresh division would probably have forced our line back and gained the shelter of Ziegler's Grove had it not been subjected to our flank fire, which destroyed its formation and sent its shattered and disordered masses along the other side of the lane [which then ran from the Bryan House to the Emmitsburg Road] and in front of the Third Division of the Second Corps.[20]

Returning to Hancock's observations, the Second Corps commander made it clear in his official report that the whole Confederate movement to the front of Webb's brigade was an adjustment, an alternate course for the divisions of both Pickett and Pettigrew. In other words, it was never the Confederate plan to place the weight of the entire charge in front of Webb and the copse of trees, as Bachelder seemed to believe it was. Hancock stated it in this way: "The right of the attacking line [Pickett's] having been repulsed by Hall's and Harrow's brigades, of the latter [2nd] division, assisted by the fire of the Vermont regiments before referred to, doubled to its left and also reinforced the center, and thus the attack was in its fullest strength opposite the brigade of General Webb."[21] The collapse of Pickett's right forced the "doubling" of that division to the left, rather than the more natural dressing left, which was intended. Likewise, the collapse of Pettigrew's left flank forced a movement for some of that division to the front of Webb. Therefore, the massing of forces to Webb's front was not a planned and willful act.

As one explores in greater depth the logic of the assault aimed toward Ziegler's Grove, one must consider the tactical importance of that location in contrast to that of the memorialized copse of trees. Colonel MacDougall of the 111th New York stated his preference for Ziegler's Grove this way:

"On examining the configuration of the ground, I assert, no student of military tactics with a practiced eye can say otherwise."[22]

MacDougall obviously possessed an advantage when he examined the terrain that cannot be enjoyed today. Cemetery Hill is now thoroughly camouflaged from the view of modern historians, a fact that has contributed to its poor status in discussions concerning its value as a strategic position. Modern structures such as the National Park Service Cyclorama and Visitor Centers, businesses along Steinwehr Avenue, and housing developments west of that street have all rendered Cemetery Hill a hidden treasure. The general contour of the hill is now more visible since the removal of the National Tower on July 3, 2000. But even so, it is still so obscured that a modern viewer is unable to observe Cemetery Hill from what would have been Lee's perspective near his headquarters around the Seminary buildings west

Perhaps the best modern view of Cemetery Hill is shown here. Taken immediately north of the North Carolina Memorial, on Seminary Ridge, the photograph shows (in masked form) the perspective of Cemetery Hill had by Pettigrew's and Trimble's men. The growth of the woods, in the foreground, has hidden the main Cemetery Hill, except in the winter when foliage is absent. The white Cyclorama building (in the background to the right) and the redbrick National Park Visitor Center (to the left) are both visible. Between these two buildings was the mature, nearly two-acre Ziegler's Grove, cut down in the 1870s or 1880s. Lee and his staff likely watched the charge from near this spot, rather than from the location of the Virginia Memorial, as is commonly believed. Note that Lee's vista from this position would have been more aligned with Ziegler's Grove.

Photograph by Lisa Harman

of the town. Without being able to see exactly what Lee saw, how can we hope to accurately assess his intentions? It is not easy to visualize Lee's view of Cemetery Hill in July 1863, but it is critical to consider this perspective when evaluating his strategy.

When carefully considering MacDougall's observation about the ground's configuration, it is fairly clear that he believed that Ziegler's Grove was on higher and more commanding ground than the officially lauded copse of trees, which was in advance of the Union position on lower ground. Specifically, MacDougall recalled that, during his postwar congressional years in Washington, D.C., "General Longstreet himself in frequent conversations I had with him said it was the grove of larger trees on the higher ground that was their aim and point of direction."[23]

In 1887 and 1888, when Bachelder was seriously contemplating Pickett's objective, "the grove of larger trees on higher ground" was not as conspicuous as Longstreet remembered them, as much of Ziegler's Grove had been felled and used for lumber. This likely was allowed to occur because Colonel Bachelder's informant, the Confederate veteran Walter Harrison, had attached no importance to the grove, and consequently, neither had Bachelder. In any case, the trees must have been removed in the 1870s or very early 1880s, because Paul D. Philippoteaux's 1884 rendition of the Gettysburg Cyclorama, which was largely based on William Tipton's photographs taken in 1882, does not show them. Meanwhile, by 1888, the copse of trees had grown up from being the mere saplings they had been in 1863. At the time of the battle, they were between eight and twelve feet tall, and possibly too small to catch the eye of General Lee, but by 1888 they were the only trees on the scene. A few lumberjacks plus several decades worth of growth of the copse of trees on Cemetery Ridge effectively altered historians' perception of Longstreet's assault of July 3, 1863. Moreover, Bachelder's preconceived notion, thanks to Colonel Harrison, that Ziegler's Grove was not important permitted such significant landscape alterations to occur.

Although the unfortunate intervention of axe and saw prevented Bachelder from accurately assessing the importance of Ziegler's Grove to the 1863 landscape, in the late 1800s when he was considering the significance of the high water mark, the greater strategic value of that grove did not reside in its relative size or height. Its importance is less related to proportion than to its proximity to Cemetery Hill. MacDougall may have realized this when he asserted the superiority of Ziegler's Grove as a position without parallel in that area. It is natural to assume that he realized a

Edwin Forbes's pen and ink drawing, "The Battle of Gettysburg," drawn from Seminary Ridge, supposedly as Pickett's Charge was unfolding. Interestingly, Forbes mentioned only two terrain features in his editorial notes: Culp's Hill and Ziegler's Grove. Culp's Hill is the high, completely wooded hill in the distant background. Ziegler's Grove consists of the thick grouping of trees on the left, and the wider stretch of trees to the right of the grove are woods located at the southern edge of Cemetery Hill. GETTYSBURG NATIONAL MILITARY PARK ARCHIVES

Confederate push toward the Union line in the direction of Ziegler's Grove would have achieved a much greater purpose than merely breaking it at the copse of trees.

For the modern historian, it is logical, even necessary, to ask some compelling questions: What could Confederate attackers have gained of lasting importance by merely breaking the Union line at Webb's position? Why should that area be considered an ultimate objective? If Cemetery Hill commanded Cemetery Ridge, then why halt at the lower position? Why not take the real high ground? Why would merely breaking the Union line there be any better than penetrating it elsewhere? Where would Pickett's division go from there if successful? If Longstreet's men were not moving upward to the summit of Cemetery Hill, did they intend to ignore the XI and I Corps artillery and infantry posted there? Was it really intended for Confederate attackers to then move directly east across Cemetery Ridge and ignore the seventy-eight Union artillery pieces posted on the hill to their left, which might be turned to fire down on them?

Would this not be especially foolish when those same guns might be taken by flank attack with a continued oblique march?

There are no reasonable answers to these questions that would indicate that the traditional copse of trees was a point of lasting tactical value. Exploration into each of the above inquiries leads only to dead ends. The bottom line is that there were no long-term gains to be made by merely breaking and holding the Union line at the copse of trees. Perhaps it could be said that if Pickett's men had broken through there, they might have divided and enfiladed the Federal battle line to the north and south, in two separate directions. The major flaw with this theory is that nearly 6,000 men of Pickett's division were diagonally facing Cemetery Hill on their approach, a fact that merely raises more questions: Why would Lee have them come at the Federals that way if he did not intend for them to follow through in that direction? Is it really conceivable that he would expect some or all of them to wheel right 180 degrees after they broke through Webb's line and advance in the opposite direction? If so, why would Pickett's troops move away from Culp's Hill, when Lee originally planned a coordinated attack with Ewell's troops there?

Other shortcomings exist in the view that Bachelder's trees were the main objective of Longstreet's assault. Another example is the notion that

---

OPPOSITE PAGE: On July 2 and 3, Confederate artillery would try to exploit the only real advantage offered by their exterior lines: the possibility of converging their artillery fire against the central position of Cemetery Hill. Longstreet indicated in his report that the central focus of his assault on July 3 was against the point where all three Confederate corps converged their artillery fire. Ewell's guns from Benner's Hill, the railroad cut, and Oak Hill were to fire on Cemetery Hill from the east and north. A. P. Hill's guns were to fire on Cemetery Hill from Seminary Ridge to the west. Finally, Longstreet's artillery was to enfilade the northern reaches of Cemetery Ridge and the main Cemetery Hill, from the southwest and west. One of the reasons Lee believed "Longstreet's Assault" could succeed on July 3 was that Confederate gunners by then controlled the Peach Orchard as an artillery platform to help bring converging fire against Cemetery Hill. Lee, believing the orchard to be "desired ground," had planned to establish this artillery position the day before, but Sickles's unanticipated forward movement had prevented this.

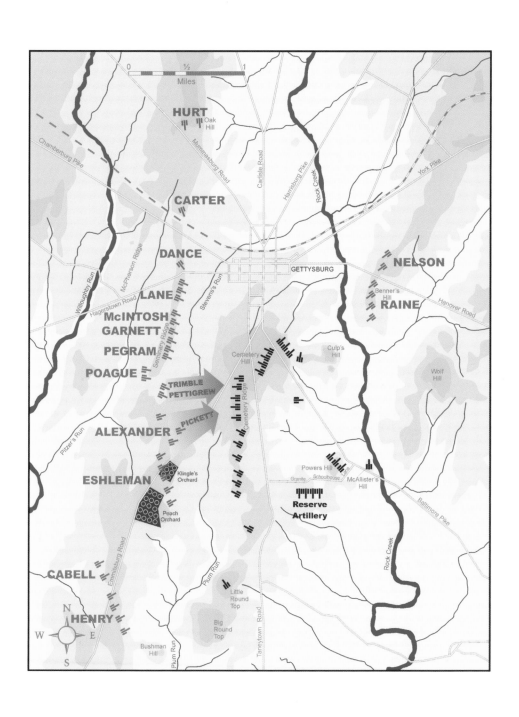

0 ½ 1
Miles

HURT
Oak Hill

CARTER

Chambersburg Pike

Mummasburg Road

Carlisle Road

Harrisburg Pike

Rock Creek

York Pike

DANCE

GETTYSBURG

NELSON

Benner's Hill

RAINE

Hanover Road

LANE

Stevens's Run

McINTOSH
GARNETT

Hagerstown Road

Seminary Ridge

Culp's Hill

Wolf Hill

PEGRAM

Cemetery Hill

POAGUE

TRIMBLE
PETTIGREW

Cemetery Ridge

PICKETT

ALEXANDER

Pitzer's Run

ESHLEMAN

Klingle's Orchard

Powers Hill

Granite Schoolhouse

McAllister's Hill

Baltimore Pike

Reserve
Artillery

Peach Orchard

CABELL

Emmitsburg Road

Plum Run

Little Round Top

Rock Creek

HENRY

N
W   E
S

Bushman Hill

Plum Run

Big Round Top

Taneytown Road

Willoughby Run

McPherson Ridge

the slight jut in the stone wall in front of Webb and his 71st Pennsylvania Infantry, roughly marked by the copse of trees, should be referred to as an "angle" in terms of its military importance. Holders of the affirmed version of the battle believe that the ninety-degree cutback in the wall was somehow a salient that could be exploited by converging fire. Was there really enough of a protrusion in Webb's line there that would warrant the attention of 12,000 attackers? Believers of this idea seem to readily accept the concept of densely stacked Confederate columns, standing side by side for a mile, focusing their attention on a bend in a wall sticking out a mere sixty-eight yards.

A second illogical notion about this deviation in the stone wall is that it faced backward to the diagonal approach of Pickett's division, which raises the question of whether this "angle" was visible from their perspective. Were Pickett's men even aware of the slight zigzag there? Walking the route of the charge today, it is difficult to distinguish the traditional angle from three-quarters of the way across the field. Visitors to the site repeatedly ask where the angle is, even as they are right upon it. The natural question that follows then is, what constitutes an angle in the sense of tactical significance? In the most literal sense, the word salient refers to something that is "prominent, striking, noticeable, and conspicuous."[24] In the case of the stone wall in front of Webb's troops, it is evident that it was, and is, barely a jut, which alone could hardly have warranted the attention of a massive assault.

There are those who will still have trouble accepting that the small angle in front of Webb's position did not mark Lee's target. Their objections are based primarily on this comment in Longstreet's report: "Orders were given to Major-General Pickett to form his line under the best cover that he could to get from the enemy's batteries, and so that the center of the assaulting column would arrive at the salient of the enemy's position, General Pickett's line to be the guide and to attack the line of the enemy's defenses, and General Pettigrew, in command of Heth's division, moving on the same line as General Pickett, was to assault the salient at the same moment."[25]

These are Longstreet's key words, to which the supporters of the affirmed history cling: "General Pettigrew . . . moving on the same line as General Pickett, was to assault the salient at the same moment."[26] These supporters also will assent to Colonel Fry's claim that his brigade, located to the right of Pettigrew's division, was the point of direction.[27] Since Fry's brigade eventually struck just to the left (or north) of Webb's angle and because Pickett came upon this position from the right, then it is presumed that Webb's position at the small angle was the objective and the salient to which Longstreet referred.

The serious shortcoming with this line of reasoning is that the full width of Pettigrew's and Trimble's line did not attack that point—a spot that only a handful of assaulting troops could have squeezed into. Since those two divisions attacked to the left of Webb's angle, and not the projection itself, it can be deduced that only a handful of their line actually found that spot, which so many assume to be the salient. In other words, in the affirmed version, Pettigrew and Trimble did not assault a salient. Instead, they attacked a normal linear battle line to the left of a sixty-eight-yard jut in the wall. As only a few of his troops, in fact, assaulted the salient, which only after the battle came to be recognized as such, Longstreet must have been describing a more substantial salient upon which his three or four divisions were to arrive "at the same moment."[28]

The only salient that was assaulted simultaneously by the men of Pickett, Pettigrew, Trimble and Anderson to a degree, was the one formed by Hancock's entire line, whose II Corps constituted one side of an angle. With this being the case, the apex of this salient was defined around Hancock's unsecured right flank, in Ziegler's Grove. Between Ziegler's Grove and Taneytown Road—a road roughly 250 yards behind and east of the grove—was formed the other side of the salient, which was to be assaulted by Col. J. M. Brockenbrough's Virginia Brigade (forming Pettigrew's left), and perhaps part of Rodes's division, whose orders were general.

Unlike the angle in front of Webb's troops, this salient would have attracted the convergence of 12,000 attackers. Tactically speaking, Hancock's right flank was unstable, or up in the air, well in front of and salient to Howard's XI Corps position to the right, and was marked by nearly two acres of mature trees interspersed with massive white oaks. Ziegler's Grove, as it was in July 1863, would have been easily visible at a distance to a first wave of 12,000 Confederate attackers—and perhaps to the second wave of 15,000 supports—on a black-powder cloudy, smoke-covered field.

In review, the point of the salient was at Ziegler's Grove, but anywhere along Hancock's forward and advance line in relation to Howard's XI Corps on his right could be referred to as the western face of the salient. The only salient that was prominent and conspicuous enough that the whole of Longstreet's columns could have "assault[ed] at the same moment" was the larger side of an angle defined by Hancock's entire offset

One of Bachelder's Troop Position Maps. Completed in the late 1870s, this particular map shows positions from 4 to 8 A.M. on July 3, 1863. Observe the conspicuous salient apex at Ziegler's Grove (between the Emanuel Trostle and Bryan Farms), which was the result of an uneven alignment between Howard's XI Corps and Hancock's II Corps. Also note the advanced position of Rodes's division, along Long Lane, whose officers waited for a "favorable opportunity" to help Wilcox, Lang, Pickett, Pettigrew, and Trimble take Cemetery Hill.

A modern view of Hancock's salient position. Looking north and northeast from the southern extension of Cemetery Ridge, the full depth and breadth of Hancock's salient at Ziegler's Grove can be appreciated. Notice the 90-degree angle formed around Ziegler's Grove on the left and down to the Wright House on the right. The Union II Corps line here is indicated by the red dotted line. This is the same perspective that Pickett's division had as they turned obliquely toward Cemetery Hill. PHOTOGRAPH BY LISA HARMAN

line. Had Brockenbrough's Virginia Brigade continued to advance, it would have been on track to strike the very point of this angle at Ziegler's Grove, and Rodes's divisional advance would have supported its left by aligning against Col. Orland Smith's brigade along Taneytown Road.

A quick clarification is needed here as to the role of General Rodes's division in Longstreet's assault. Rodes was given "general orders," which implied there was to be an attack along the whole of the enemy's line, should the opportunity occur. Rodes reported not only that his orders were "general" for July 3, but also that they were "the same as those of the day before."[29] He stated that his orders from the day before required him to "co-operate with the attacking force as soon as any opportunity of doing so with good effect was offered."[30] Specifically concerning July 3, he recorded:

> We were on the lookout for another favorable opportunity to co-operate. When the sound of musketry was heard, it became apparent that the enemy in our front was much excited. The favorable opportunity seemed to

me close at hand. I sent word to Lieutenant-General
Ewell by Major [H. A.] Whiting, of my staff, that in a few
moments I should attack, and immediately had my handful of men, under [brigade commanders] Doles, Iverson,
and Ramseur, prepared for the onset; but in less than five
minutes after Major Whiting's departure, before the
troops on my immediate right had made any advance or
showed any preparation therefore, and just as the order
forward was about to be given to my line, it was an-
nounced, and was apparent to me, that the attack had already failed.[31]

Rodes's men were "on the lookout for another favorable opportunity to
cooperate."[32] Again, if Rodes had proceeded from Long Lane, some of his
line would have supported Brockenbrough on his left in the attempt to turn
Hancock's right flank at the salient apex of Ziegler's Grove. However, much
of Rodes's attacking force would have moved against Colonel Smith's
brigade at Taneytown Road. One must assume that at some point, Rodes
and Brockenbrough would have needed the involvement of Col. Abner
Perrin's (McGowan's) South Carolina Brigade and Brig. Gen. Edward L.
Thomas's Georgia Brigade to bridge the gaps and fill in the line. Both of
these brigades of Pender's division were in an advanced position to the
right of Rodes and to the left front of Brockenbrough and were likely the
troops that Rodes referred to on his "immediate right" that were not ready
to advance.

So then, according to plan, perhaps, Colonel Smith's brigade, joined
by the remnants of Col. Charles R. Coster's brigade, also of the XI Corps,
should have felt Pickett's oblique push toward their position, from their
left, while Rodes threatened their front. As Pickett's men proceeded
obliquely into Ziegler's Grove, joining Pettigrew's and Trimble's men, Confederate attackers would have enjoyed the shelter that the grove provided
against Union artillery fire from Cemetery Hill, and that would have
shielded them in their attempt to seize the "main position, the Cemetery
Hill."[33] Bachelder's traditional copse of trees barely offered shade, much
less this kind of protection.

An opponent of this line of reasoning might well contend that Longstreet's report also states that "the center of the assaulting column would
arrive at the salient of the enemy's position."[34] The reasoning then follows

A modern photograph of Garnett's route in the field of Pickett's Charge. Observe the distinctiveness of Ziegler's Grove, which aligns directly with the course charted by the left of Garnett and Armistead. Cornfields, which did not exist on this part of the field in July 1863, are visible to the left and right of Ziegler's Grove. A path has been cut through the corn, and is maintained so that visitors may precisely follow Pickett's "left oblique," which lines up perfectly with the grove. Also note the low, troughlike swale in the foreground. Armistead's brigade stopped here to dress their lines in the middle of the charge. The spot where this photograph was taken is likely where Garnett's brigade began to connect with Pettigrew's division, which would have moved from left to right here. Photograph by Lisa Harman

that if Fry's brigade pointed the direction, from the center of Longstreet's assault toward the immediate left of Webb's angle, then the true salient must have been to Fry's right front. The problem with this logic is that Longstreet was unaware that Fry believed his brigade to be the one indicating the direction. To read Longstreet's report is to believe that it was not part of his orders to have everyone move on Fry. Longstreet stated that "General Pickett's line [was] to be the guide,"[35] and that he was to guide in such a way that "the center of the assaulting column would arrive at the salient of the enemy's position."[36]

Perhaps Longstreet meant for Pickett's division to guide but his orders were changed, without his knowledge or permission, at the brigade level. In this case, when Longstreet stated that the "center of the assaulting column" was to "arrive at the salient," perhaps he originally meant for Pickett's "center" to be the point of direction. In later years, Longstreet added that "the divisions [of Pettigrew and Trimble] of the Third Corps were arranged along his [Pickett's] left with orders to take up the line of march, as Picket passed before them."[37] In this picture, Pickett's division is clearly described as the guide and director. This picture also fits with where General Lee watched the charge, which was from Pettigrew's position, "about 200 yards" north of the present-day Virginia memorial. His post of command, including his staff, was probably on a high slope situated at the present-day North Carolina memorial, which, interestingly, is across from Ziegler's Grove. From there, perhaps, he expected to see Pickett pass before him.[38] For whatever reasons, most of Longstreet's writings reveal that he viewed the participation of A. P. Hill's divisions as secondary to the outcome. It is therefore unlikely that Longstreet looked to Hill for direction.

Without the reports of Generals Pickett, Pettigrew, Garnett, Kemper, Armistead, and numerous colonels who participated in the charge, it may never be known with absolute certainty which terrain feature Pickett's men were aiming toward. But even today, if one walks the left oblique from any part of Pickett's front, he will find that Ziegler's Grove prominently centers with that front on a forty-five-degree course. In fact, if one strictly adheres to the forty-five-degree turn during his walk, allowing for the full maturation of the turn, he will discover that Bachelder's copse of trees would have demanded much of Garnett's brigade to break the oblique maneuver, with an awkward veer to the right.

There is certainly room to advance this line of reasoning a bit further. If the truth were to be known, really any part of Pickett's line could have guided the assault, as all of his regiments would have found the point of the sizable salient, at Ziegler's Grove, directly in their sights. Garnett's left regiments especially would have found this to be true, as their forty-five-degree course was perfectly charted toward the grove.

CHAPTER 10

Who Directed
Pickett's Charge?

As one digs deeper into this matter, it becomes more and more complicated to insist that Colonel Fry's brigade on Pettigrew's right guided
Pickett's Charge. This difficulty arises from the fact that Pettigrew and
Pickett approached Cemetery Hill and Cemetery Ridge from two different
directions. Pettigrew marched straight across the field, whereas Pickett
came toward the Union line at a forty-five-degree angle or at nearly ninety
degrees in relation to the Emmitsburg Road. In layman's terms, Pettigrew
was to be the "left jab" and Pickett the "right hook."

The thought of the assault guiding on Fry's brigade conjures up an
image of Pickett's left marching alongside Fry's right as they crossed the
fields. In actuality, the picture should be one of Pickett's men moving perpendicular to Fry's men. Because Pickett's division approached Pettigrew's
division at nearly right angles, the point at which the former intersected
the latter became a somewhat awkward mixing point. Garnett's and Fry's
brigades, of these two divisions, did become crisscrossed and intertwined in
front of the Union position.

One might wonder why Fry would claim that he had guided the charge
if he had not in fact done so. One factor that must be considered is the time
that elapsed between the event and Fry's written account of it. Because of
the severe wound he suffered during Longstreet's assault, Fry did not write
an official report while the thoughts of battle were still fresh in his mind.
Rather, his most influential written version of the charge was recounted

fifteen years after the event. At that time, the chairman of the Executive Committee of the Southern Historical Society, Dabney H. Maury, had pleaded with Fry to "vindicate the good name of those troops and the fair name of Pettigrew."[1] Such a request carried with it a lot of responsibility, and it probably weighed heavily on Fry. Perhaps after much thought, and feeling the pressure to exonerate, Fry stretched his story to claim that "from the commencement of the advance to the closing death grapple, his [Pettigrew's] right brigade [of Fry] was the directing one."[2]

Although this claim was made under pressure years after the event, it is still fairly straightforward and deserving of scrutiny. Upon closer investigation, however, it becomes clear that there are other, more fundamental shortcomings with Fry's claim that his brigade directed the charge, not the least of which is the issue of his premature exit from the fight. Shortly after hearing Garnett yell to him that he was dressing on his brigade, Fry noted that Garnett "fell dead." Fry stated, "A moment later . . . a shot through the thigh prostrated me." Fry then shouted to his men, "Go on . . . [and] The men rushed forward into the smoke, which soon became so dense that I could see little of what was going on before me."[3]

In his prostrated condition, surrounded by dense smoke, how could Fry possibly be sure that his brigade led the way? The easiest way to confirm Fry's claim is to check the report of his successor, Lt. Col. S. G. Shepard of the 7th Tennessee Infantry. Shepard, who assumed leadership of the brigade after Fry was wounded, should confirm Fry's claims, but he does not. In his report, Shepard seemed to possess no knowledge that his brigade was directing the assault. Instead, he discusses the problem of Pickett's and Pettigrew's lines "not being an exact continuation of each other. . . . The command was then passed down the line by the officers, 'Guide right'; and we advanced our right, guiding by General Pickett's left." As to the validity of this account, Shepard avows, "Upon my own observation and the testimony of the officers of each of the regiments I predicate my statements."[4]

Surely at least some of the officers that Shepard conferred with would have known their brigade was directing the assault if in fact it was. One of the officers with whom Shepard may have consulted was Capt. J. B. Turney of Company K, 1st Tennessee Infantry. It was Turney's regiment that connected with Garnett's brigade of Pickett's division. Nowhere in Turney's detailed postwar account does he allude to the issue that their brigade was directing the assault. The only clue he gives about the destination of the charge was that "Cemetery Hill was the chief objective point, and along its crest and behind a stone wall rested the Federal center."[5] Not only did critical witnesses from Fry's own brigade, such as Shepard and Turney, fail to support his assertions, but so too did Maj. Charles S. Peyton, who took over command of Garnett's brigade. Major Peyton, whose Virginia Brigade connected with Fry's brigade, made no mention of being obligated to Colonel Fry for direction.[6]

Much uncertainty continues to surround the question of who charted the direction of the charge. In her groundbreaking work, *Pickett's Charge in History and Memory*, historian Carol Reardon summarizes, "Since Pickett and Pettigrew would march forth on different axes of advance, cooperation was essential to success, but history is relatively silent on measures taken by any senior leader to assure that troops from two different corps could coordinate their actions in the heat of battle."[7] Reardon's points are significant in that she breaks with the affirmed version of events by calling attention to the relative difficulty of two divisions traveling on different axes coordinating an attack, and to the lack of evidence relating to any single individual directing the maneuver. Because it focuses more on the futility of the assault than on its technical feasibility, the affirmed story never goes beyond the image of both divisions marching side by side in virtually a straight line.

One other basic weakness with Fry's claim is that he never mentioned where his brigade was aiming. It is odd that Fry asserted that he directed the way but then did not disclose his target. That he was marching toward a copse of trees is the assumption of others, and not a claim that he made. Where was he going? If he was targeting Bachelder's copse of trees, he missed them anyway.

Perhaps Fry's true role was to ensure that Pettigrew's division connected with Pickett's division. This would explain why other brigades to his left and right dressed toward him. That the other brigades "dressed" or "aligned" on his fits better with Fry's original claims to Bachelder.[8] "Dress" and "align" are important distinctions, because they have more to do with connection than direction. In reality, Pettigrew's brigades to the left of Fry were dressing on Pickett (as they, in turn, dressed on Fry). Likewise, Pickett's brigades dressed left merely to connect with Pettigrew, and not for the purpose of direction. Since Longstreet told Pickett to guide, there would have been no need to depend on Fry to chart a course.

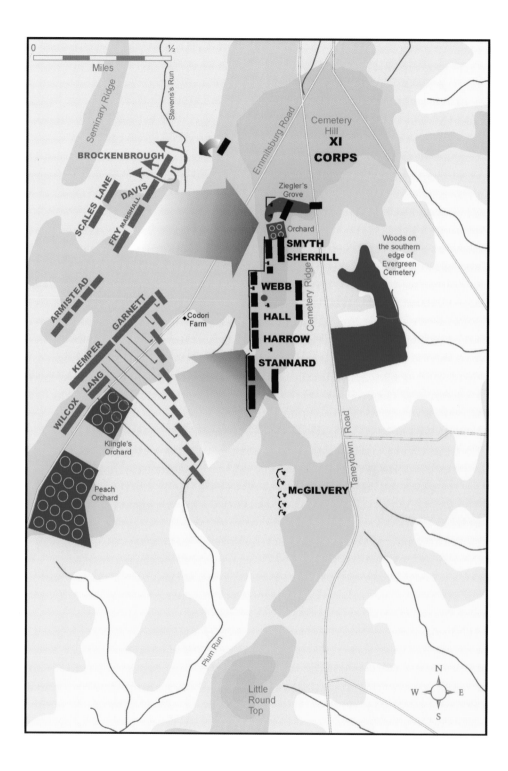

One further thought regarding the direction of the assault is a matter of semantics. When Longstreet stated that the assaulting column was to move "on the same line," he may have been using "on" in the sense of "against" and "line" to refer to the Union line. Thus he would have meant that the assaulting column was to move against the same section of Union line.[9] I tend to believe this interpretation of the sentence is a bit of a stretch, but that overall the evidence is clear that Longstreet meant for Pickett to guide and for Pettigrew to parlay off that movement.

Longstreet made one other key statement related to the point of direction for the assault. In his official report, he recorded, "All of the [Confederate] batteries of the First [Longstreet's] and Third [Hill's] Corps, and some of those of the Second [Ewell's], were put into the best positions for effective

---

OPPOSITE PAGE: In the fighting on July 3, Pettigrew and Trimble constituted the Confederate "left jab" while Pickett represented the "right hook." Notice the advanced, unprotected right flank of Hancock's line, which ended abruptly at Ziegler's Grove. This is likely the point of the salient that Lee saw from his headquarters directly opposite at Seminary Ridge. With the salient point at Ziegler's Grove, one side of this angle was represented by the extension south of Hancock's line. The other side of this angle extended 250 yards east of Ziegler's Grove to the Taneytown Road, where Union I and XI Corps troops defended. Brockenbrough's Virginia Brigade was on course to attack this very point, and the officers of Rodes's division were looking for a "favorable opportunity" to come up on their left. At the other end of the Confederate line, Pickett was supposed to be supported more closely, on his right, by Wilcox and Lang. Additionally, their right was to be followed and protected by a mass of Confederate artillery, which would have been available had not ammunition supplies been depleted by an extended precharge cannonade. Had Pickett's right flank been protected this way as designed, then his division should have flanked Stannard's Vermonters on Cemetery Ridge. Having done so, they might have driven them by flank to the front of Pettigrew and toward Cemetery Hill. Last, observe that Pickett's troops formed nearly a 90-degree angle with the Emmitsburg Road as they emulated Hood's assault "up the Emmitsburg Road" from the day before. The only difference between Hood's attack and Pickett's was that Pickett's assault was deployed closer to the goal of Cemetery Hill.

fire upon the point of attack."[10] What was Longstreet saying? He was conveying that all available Confederate batteries from all three Confederate corps attempted to converge their fire upon the point of attack for Longstreet's assault. Was there a common position fired upon by all three Confederate corps' batteries? The few guns of Ewell's artillery, which fired on July 3 during the great cannonade, clearly fired against the eastern and northern faces of Cemetery Hill. Perhaps four fired there from Benner's Hill east of town, while others fired from Oak Hill and the railroad cut north of Gettysburg. All of A. P. Hill's guns fired from the west along Seminary Ridge against Maj. Thomas W. Osborn's XI Corps artillery brigade, located along the western face of Cemetery Hill. Finally, the guns of Longstreet's corps fired mostly from southwest to northeast, from a slanted position, against Union artillery along the northernmost portions of Cemetery Ridge and the southwest hillock of Cemetery Hill, marked by Ziegler's Grove.

Since it can be safely assumed that Confederate artillery from all three corps were attempting to converge their fire, and since the only point where their fire overlapped or intersected was Cemetery Hill, then the overall hill must have been Longstreet's "point of attack."[11] If there were any remaining doubts as to where the artillery fire was to converge, Longstreet dispelled them in a reprint article sent to the Southern Historical Society in 1878, in which he specified, "Our artillery was to be massed . . . and it was to pour a continuous fire upon the cemetery."[12] Lee's military secretary, A. L. Long, who was with the general that day, concurred that "the signal for battle was given, which was immediately followed by the concentrated fire of all the Confederate artillery on Cemetery Hill."[13]

One additional line of argument that favors the Ziegler's Grove area as the target for the charge relates to the significant Union activity there on the evening of July 2. There is so much said about a gap in the Union center below the traditional "copse of trees," which General Wright's Georgia Brigade penetrated on the evening of July 2, that it is deduced that Longstreet's assault on July 3 was destined for that perceived gap, and for the copse of trees nearby.

That the gap there figured into Lee's reasoning for an assault is very likely. However, a far greater gap opened in Ziegler's Grove on the evening of July 2. In fact, no less than the equivalent of three Union brigades abandoned the grove for other contested areas. From Hays's division of the II Corps, Col. Samuel S. Carroll's brigade moved from the grove to East

Cemetery Hill, and Col. George L. Willard's brigade shifted from the grove south to Codori thicket, while Maj. Gen. Carl Schurz shifted his brigade-size XI Corps division from the northeastern reaches of the grove over to East Cemetery Hill and Culp's Hill. Perhaps as many as 4,200 fighting men abandoned Ziegler's Grove in the growing dusk of late July 2.

From his headquarters adjacent to the Seminary, Lee must have looked directly across to Ziegler's Grove and observed some of this dramatic activity. It would have seemed logical to him that if he could arrange coordinated attacks against Culp's Hill from the east and Cemetery Hill from the west on July 3, then Ziegler's Grove might empty again. This time, with proper coordination, he might take full advantage. Indeed, Lee's official reports clearly spelled out that he expected Pickett's three brigades to attack the next morning in concert with Ewell's forces at Culp's Hill. If one takes into account all of the Union troops that exited Cemetery Ridge and the western half of Cemetery Hill during the evening of July 2, including Caldwell's entire 1st Division, is it any wonder that Lee would believe that Hancock's entire II Corps line was suspect, even vulnerable, to a proper concert of action? Fortunately for Hancock, Sedgwick's VI Corps arrived in time, late on July 2, to insulate Meade's whole line for July 3. In retrospect, unbeknownst to Lee, a proper concert of action on July 3 could not produce the same movement away from Cemetery Ridge after Sedgwick's arrival.

A compromise can be reached between those who see Bachelder's copse of trees as the key terrain feature and those who choose Ziegler's Grove. It comes easily enough if one pictures correctly the approach that Pickett's division made: The men marched toward Cemetery Hill and Ridge at a forty-five-degree angle, rather than directly, as everyone seems to imagine. In this case, an oblique course would have permitted these two separate groupings of trees to connect on the same line. They do line up, along an oblique route, toward Cemetery Hill.

CONCLUSION

The third and final day of battle closed with Lee still not able to seize Cemetery Hill. Union artillery at Powers Hill on the Baltimore Pike, amounting to a preemptive Union attack, forced Ewell to fight at Culp's Hill during the morning of July 3, before Longstreet was in position to assault the western side of the Cemetery Hill salient. The result was that Meade's army defeated Lee's "general plan," both in sequence and in detail.

Sharing the death and defeat with Lee's army that day was the "ephemeral event" that held the truth of Lee's general plan. As memory of the ephemeral event began to fade over the subsequent decades, the "affirmed event" gradually replaced it. By the twenty-fifth anniversary, the narrative of the battle did not reveal a Confederate general plan or any single tactical objective pursued by Lee. Over the decades that followed, Lee's one objective was multiplied into many different objectives, each of them created by those who wished to advance their own favored scenario or military unit.

If there is any semblance of a general plan that is accepted today, it is that Lee assaulted both Union flanks on July 2, and then changed his plan for July 3 to a direct frontal assault against the Union center. This scenario is not a general plan, however, but a radical shift in focus from one day to the next. To conclude that Lee floundered for three days of battle without designating a single, focused objective is to believe that the Confederate commanding general either forgot or ignored the most elementary principles of warfare, in which he had spent a lifetime of training. The affirmed version of the battle endorses this extremely unlikely conclusion.

There were several distinct shifts in the post–Civil War years that contributed to the obscuring of Lee's general plan. The first, and most identifiable, involved controversies surrounding both Sickles and Longstreet after the war. Both, for various reasons, were considered the "black sheep" of their armies, which caused their veteran peers to scrutinize their participation at Gettysburg. Sickles's acceptance of the prestigious Medal of Honor in 1897 for his efforts at Gettysburg added to the existing resentment against him. This animosity fostered debates about whether Sickles had directly disobeyed Meade's orders by advancing to the Peach Orchard on July 2. At the heart of the criticism was his inability to cover Little Round Top, giving rise to other arguments about who should have received credit for saving that precipice. By 1913, Oliver Norton had collected and published many of these compelling accounts in *The Attack and Defense of Little Round Top: Gettysburg, July 2, 1863.*

Longstreet became mired in similar political turmoil after the war, along with trouble created by his criticism of the late Gen. Robert E. Lee. Longstreet was perceived as a traitor by some members of the Southern elite, who felt that his obstinacy toward Lee at Gettysburg contributed greatly to the commanding general's defeat. Resentment and bitterness, shared by several former Confederate officers, led to a microscopic reevaluation of Longstreet's actions at Gettysburg—a battle that came to be considered the turning point of the Civil War.

Because of the veterans' severe criticism of Sickles and Longstreet for their actions on July 2, an inadvertent spotlight was placed on the portion of the battlefield on which they had participated. Since these controversies were so thoroughly reexamined around the time of the battle's twenty-fifth anniversary in the 1880s, then it was perhaps at this point that the battle's historiography shifted toward a disproportionate emphasis on the importance of Little Round Top. Cemetery Hill, which was treated with such importance immediately after the battle as the location of the Soldiers' National Cemetery and as the meeting place of several early reunions, seemed to assume a secondary role to Little Round Top by that time. It is probably no coincidence, therefore, that it was as late as 1893 that Col. Joshua Chamberlain of the 20th Maine received the Medal of Honor for helping to save Little Round Top. Attention had shifted to Chamberlain only when emphasis in the battle's historiography had moved to Little Round Top.

The building of a trolley car system on the battlefield in the late 1880s and early 1890s further detracted from Cemetery Hill's place in the battle's history. By the 1890s, veterans and visitors arriving in Gettysburg by train could transfer downtown onto a trolley designed to carry them in the direction of the Round Tops. With the trolley in place, the southern portions of the battlefield became considerably more accessible, more publicized, and therefore eventually more important. East Cemetery Hill became the last stop on the tour, and Culp's Hill was excluded from the trolley route altogether. By the 1890s, they drew the attention of only the more intrepid visitors. Prior to the trolley's construction, Cemetery Hill and Culp's Hill were the two most prominent Union positions that were in easy walking distance from the town, and therefore the most often visited. The trolley made Cemetery Hill only one of many stops.

This occurred in addition to the felling of Ziegler's Grove in the late 1870s to early 1880s, which had significantly altered the 1863 landscape. It was only after the removal of this grove that Bachelder's copse of trees started to gain recognition in the Pickett's Charge story line. Without Ziegler's Grove to mark the western face of Cemetery Hill, the intent and direction of the charge became less clear.

Hand in hand with all of the above misfortune was the deemphasis of the roles of Pettigrew and Trimble in the charge. Generations of military historians have recognized that the July 3 attack should rightfully be referred to as "Longstreet's Assault," yet the misnomer of "Pickett's Charge" has remained. Why is this so? According to some of the veterans of Pettigrew's brigade, their reputations suffered at the hands of some of Pickett's men, who shaped their own story in the American mind.

The trouble may have begun with the denial of a request General Lee had made to the Confederate secretary of war on September 8, 1863, in which Lee stated that he believed "it would be better to have no correspondents of the press with the army."[1] His strict request was perhaps in reaction to a leak to the press appearing in a Williamsport, Maryland, newspaper after the battle, in which a Confederate informant blamed the failure of the charge on the premature retreat of Pettigrew's North Carolina troops. A similar leak occurred at Gettysburg to a Richmond newspaper that greatly harmed the reputation of Pettigrew's men. Apparently, many of that division believed that had the secretary of war complied with Lee's wishes in September 1863, damage might have been spared them, as the stories mounted with time. By the time Pettigrew's men systematically responded to these accusations in the postwar years, it was too late to clear their names. Pickett's version of the charge, which heralded the Virginians over the North Carolinians, had triumphed. Consequently, Pettigrew and Trimble were relegated to the subplot of the battle.

The legacy of all this has been the further downplaying of the significance of Ziegler's Grove, which was directly in the forward path of these two divisions. This has also led to significant physical alterations across the western face of Cemetery Hill. The construction of the National Park Visitor Center between the 1920s and 1960s and the Cyclorama Center by 1962, as well as the commercial development along Steinwehr Avenue, have all but obliterated the original landscape of the battle in this area. Preservation has focused only on the area where Pickett's division attacked. Ziegler's Grove, which marked the area of Hancock's unsecured right flank, and Cemetery Hill itself, sat in the direct path of Pettigrew and Trimble, yet modern development has rendered a verdict that the terrain there is not as important.[2]

Another significant occurrence that contributed to the obfuscation of Lee's general plan was the appropriation of Cemetery Hill for the Soldiers' National Cemetery. On November 19, 1863, Abraham Lincoln gave his famous Gettysburg Address at the dedication of the cemetery, calling for "a new birth of freedom." From that day forward, this commanding hill became less known for its tactical significance during the battle, and remembered more as a "final resting place for those who here gave their lives that that nation might live."[3]

The association of Cemetery Hill with Lincoln's famous speech, as the resting place of "the honored dead," has so overshadowed its original military significance that the average visitor to Gettysburg is at a loss to understand why cannons and regimental markers coexist there with burial plots. The tragic consequence has been that battlefield preservation over the last 100 years has not diligently sought to protect the northern and western slopes of the hill. Today it is difficult to see its contour, with all of the asphalt, businesses, and transplanted trees that cover it. At best, Cemetery Hill is only a shadow of its former self. It is hard to imagine that the National Cemetery organizer, David Wills, once called Cemetery Hill "the key to the whole line of our [Union] defenses,—the apex of the triangular line of battle."[4]

Looking east from the Pennsylvania Army National Guard Armory Building (along Seminary Ridge), one can now only see glimpses of the western slope of Cemetery Hill. The stadium lights, between the tree on the right and the brick armory, are those of the modern recreation park. Between the two trees, in the distant background, is the New York State monument, on the northern edge of the National Cemetery. The western slope of Cemetery Hill begins in front of the area marked by the stadium lights, below at Stevens Run. At the time of the battle, there would have been no trees, buildings, or poles in this view. On July 3, 1863, three brigades of Maj. Gen. Robert Rodes's division waited for a "favorable opportunity" to attack, from the vicinity of the stadium lights. The vantage point of this photograph also marks the location of A. P. Hill's corps artillery on July 2 and 3. PHOTOGRAPH BY LISA HARMAN

Another factor that helped to steer the battle's historiography away from the relationship between Lee and Cemetery Hill was the unfortunate loss of so many key Southern participants who might have given accounts. Had certain individuals in Lee's army survived, his general plan would have been conveyed much more clearly, through both their reports and their postwar writings. From Pickett's division alone, the historian is in want of reports from all three brigade commanders, Kemper, Garnett, and Armistead, as well as that of Major General Pickett himself. Additionally, Brigadier General Pettigrew, who commanded a substantial portion of the attacking troops on Pickett's left, subsequently died from a wound suffered during the retreat to Virginia. Equally devastating to the battle's story line was the death of Robert Rodes in the Shenandoah Valley in 1864; A. P. Hill outside of Petersburg in 1865; George Willard on July 2, 1863, at Gettysburg; and Alexander Hays at the Wilderness in 1864. Each of these articulate men might have elaborated in postwar writings on the specifics of the July 3 attack, especially in regard to Ziegler's Grove. Without the input of such crucial witnesses, it is understandable that there has been so much difficulty in re-creating the direction and purpose of "Pickett's Charge."

A further development that shifted the emphasis away from Lee's intent to seize Cemetery Hill has been the regrettable preoccupation of both veterans and historians with the "Lee versus Longstreet" controversy. Postwar Confederate writings so indulged in such arguments that discussions of the focus of the battle too often degenerated into the airing of personal grievances. The modern historian could have benefited immensely if the Confederate veterans' emphasis had been less on who was at fault for the Gettysburg defeat and more on the specifics of Lee's objective.

The somewhat blemished reputation of the Union XI Corps undoubtedly diminished the Union emphasis of Cemetery Hill as a central point for Lee's plan. It was the XI Corps that largely bore the blame for the collapse of the Union line north and west of the town of Gettysburg during the afternoon of July 1. Previously, the XI Corps had been blamed for failures in the Shenandoah Valley while challenging Stonewall Jackson there in 1862, as well as at Chancellorsville in May 1863. Added to this was a very real prejudice within the Union army, especially among its officers, toward the many German immigrants in that corps. This bias is easily recognizable in Union accounts of the battle. Perhaps other Union corps commanders realized that if they emphasized the importance of Cemetery Hill in the overall scheme of the battle, it would only draw attention to a scorned body of men in the Union army.

One final explanation for why the focus of the battle's historiography veered away from Lee's general plan to take Cemetery Hill is that his plan never matured. Lee's real plan for Gettysburg was defeated so effectively that its particulars never were completely revealed. If, on the other hand, Longstreet had been able to successfully drive in the Union left obliquely toward Cemetery Hill on July 2, no questions would have arisen about Lee's intent and focus. As had occurred before at Chancellorsville, his two wings would have converged, Cemetery Hill would have been taken, and that would have settled the issue. With his failure at Gettysburg, Lee likely saw little use after the war in rehashing Confederate shortcomings. Certainly his silence on these specific issues, in part due to his early death, further served to bury his intentions.

For all these reasons, Lee's true tactical focus for the battle of Gettysburg has remained obscured. He probably died with the knowledge that his intentions at Gettysburg were never fully understood, but saw no purpose in reviving a dead issue, especially when the defeated Confederacy had more pressing concerns at hand. Lee was not the type of man to spend much time explaining himself, anyway. Perhaps in postwar private conversations with trusted friends, he discussed events in more detail. Otherwise he appeared to be mute toward a subject that must have remained painful for him.

The few fragments of information about Gettysburg that Lee did relate before his death were to William Allen in 1868, but this information is not revealing. Possibly Lee did have aspirations of clearing up particulars about Gettysburg, such as his belief that Cemetery Hill was the key position. But even if he did, his efforts were hindered by the Federal War Department, which denied Lee (and all Southern writers) access to official documents, even those he had written himself. As historian Glenn Tucker points out: "This blackout continued for thirteen years after the end of hostilities, a period during which most of the abiding impressions about the war were being formed. It is an amazing fact that when General Robert E. Lee endeavored to inspect his own reports of battles and his own field returns, he was denied the right. He never did have the opportunity to make use of them."[5] Tucker continued: "After the war the South was virtually destitute of papers and reports bearing on the conflict. All documents either had been destroyed or had been seized by the invading armies and bundled and sent to Washington. There many of them remain. . . . The battle flags were returned long ago, but not the archives."[6]

As any historian will attest, notes are essential to compiling as complete and accurate a historical record as is possible. They jog the memory and bring back details that would otherwise be glossed over. Without his notes, the particulars of the battle of Gettysburg were apt to become fuzzy to Lee, especially as he tried to reflect from the vantage point of two or three years after the war on the many battles he had engineered. Perhaps his thoughts drifted back to the "turning point" from time to time. In these moments, he may have wondered whether, "with [Stonewall] Jackson alive and [J. E. B.] Stuart near and in his old form, the battle would not have been fought against Cemetery Hill."[7]

The affirmed story of the battle of Gettysburg has left the historian with lingering questions, the answers to which do not fully explain a general plan under which Lee claimed to have operated. Questions relating to the second and third days of the battle should be especially gnawing at the battlefield historian. For July 2, several imponderables are raised: Why was Hood ordered to attack up, and not across, the Emmittsburg Road, even after it was apparent that the Union position there was far more elaborate than was anticipated? Why was attacking in that direction so essential to Lee's plan? Why was Lee uninterested in marching around the Union left flank? Why did Lee identify the Peach Orchard, instead of Little Round Top, as the "desired ground" along the Union left? Why did Lee want Longstreet to "partially envelop the Union left" if Little Round Top was supposed to be important to his plan? If Longstreet's goal on July 2 was to "reach the crest of the ridge," which was "massed with artillery," then where does Little Round Top fit in—or does it?

For July 3, the affirmed story of Gettysburg raises just as many questions: If Pickett's Charge was planned on July 3 as a separate massive frontal assault against the Union center, then why did Lee state (in January 1864, after nearly six months of reflection) that "the general plan was unchanged" from July 2? Why did Ewell bolster Culp's Hill by nearly 6,000 enlisted men and officers, and Lee strengthen that general's rear by 8,000 cavalry, if these two men expected the fighting there to be an unrelated sideshow? Why did Ewell's troops fight for seven and a half hours at Culp's Hill that morning if they were not holding out for the cooperation of Longstreet's troops?

On the final day of the battle, further questions arise: If Longstreet, who directed Pickett's Charge, and Hancock, who defended against it, both stated clearly that Cemetery Hill was the goal of the assault, then why has the copse of trees not been more seriously called into question as being off target, or at least short of the mark? If the traditional copse of trees was the aiming point, then why did Pettigrew not order his troops to make a right oblique, which is what they needed to do to arrive there in force and by design? If merely driving a wedge into Webb's position was the goal of Pickett's Charge, then where were the attackers supposed to advance from there? What would that have accomplished? What was so strategically significant about that part of Cemetery Ridge that it should be set apart as a position that, if taken, should determine the fate of the battle?

The answers to each of these questions will remain separate, disjointed, and incompatible with each other until the central piece of the puzzle is put in place. As long as the battle's historiography wrongly revolves around Little Round Top and the copse of trees, Lee's intentions are destined to remain hidden. Until it is understood that Cemetery Hill was the bull's-eye in Lee's general plan, from at least the evening of July 1 through the remainder of the battle, the other pieces of the puzzle will never fit together.

NOTES

INTRODUCTION

1. Ernst Breisach, *Historiography: Ancient, Medieval, and Modern*, 2nd ed. (Chicago: University of Chicago Press, 1994), 331–32.

2. See David G. Martin, *Gettysburg: July 1*, rev. ed. (Conshohocken, Pa: Combined Books, 1996). Martin's revision reveals that he is to be commended for collecting and assimilating an impressive amount of information. His work is written in a straightforward, military style with each battle action described in its proper chronology. Although his mammoth undertaking explained *how* the July 1 battle unfolded, it rarely addressed *why*.

3. See Warren W. Hassler, Jr., *Crisis at the Crossroads: The First Day at Gettysburg* (Tuscaloosa: University of Alabama Press, 1970). Hassler did address the issue of why Lee's army was in the vicinity of Gettysburg on July 1 (pages 21 and 22), with his statements about Gettysburg being a vital road hub. Unfortunately, his explanation constituted only one small paragraph. Worse still, he did not return to that explanation until chapter 15, page 140. Hassler was more preoccupied with explaining the *hows* of the July 1 fighting.

4. Harry W. Pfanz, *Gettysburg: The Second Day* (Chapel Hill: University of North Carolina Press, 1987), 425. Pfanz is perhaps the most prominent of many historians of the second day's battle who believe that Sickles's forward movement was ill conceived. He wrote that "General

Sickles increased the odds of Confederate success when he advanced his Third Corps from its important and relatively secure position on Cemetery Ridge. In doing so he had abandoned vital terrain, isolated his corps, and put the entire army at special risk. It was a grievous error." With this said, let it be made clear that Harry Pfanz is the historian's historian, and it is a rare occurrence where issue might be taken with him on a particular point.

5. Kent Gramm, *Gettysburg: A Meditation on War and Values* (Bloomington: Indiana University Press, 1994), 116.

6. Edwin B. Coddington, *The Gettysburg Campaign: A Study in Command* (Dayton, Ohio: Morningside Bookshop, 1979), 458.

7. George R. Stewart, *Pickett's Charge: A Micro-history of the Final Attack at Gettysburg, July 3, 1863* (Cambridge, Mass.: Riverside, 1959), 21.

8. Glen Tucker, *High Tide at Gettysburg: The Campaign in Pennsylvania* (1958; reprint, Gettysburg: Stan Clark Military Books, 1995), 333.

9. William Garrett Piston, "Cross Purposes: Longstreet, Lee, and Confederate Attack Plans for July 3 at Gettysburg," in *The Third Day at Gettysburg and Beyond*, ed. Gary W. Gallagher (Chapel Hill: University of North Carolina Press, 1994), 35. Had Piston realized that Cemetery Hill was the objective of Lee's concentric battle plan, his essay would have been complete.

10. Robert E. Lee, "Report of July 31, 1863," and "Report of January __, 1864," *War of the Rebellion: Official Records* (Washington, D.C.: Government Printing Office, 1889), vol. 27, ser. 1, pt. 2, 308, 320. Hereafter, all notations to the *Official Records*—cited as OR—will not include the series or volume numbers since they remain the same for each of the three parts in the Gettysburg set. Part 1 is Union, while part 2 is Confederate, and part 3 is Correspondence.

11. Lee, "Report of January __, 1864," OR pt. 2, 320. Also see Richard S. Ewell, "Report of __ __, 1863," OR pt. 2, 447. Ewell states, "And when too late to recall [Johnson], I received notice that Longstreet would not attack until 10 o'clock; but as it turned out, his attack was delayed till after 2 o'clock.

CHAPTER 1

1. Frank L. Byrne and Andrew T. Weaver, eds., *Haskell of Gettysburg: His Life and Civil War Papers* (Madison: State Historical Society of Wisconsin, 1970), 94.

2. Jeffry D. Wert, *General James Longstreet: The Confederacy's Most Controversial Soldier: A Biography* (New York: Simon and Schuster, 1996), 266.

3. Conrad H. Lanza, *Napoleon and Modern War: His Military Maxims,* rev. ed. (Harrisburg, Pa.: Military Service, 1943), 67. Lee belonged to the "Napoleon Club" when he was at West Point. The club was mostly a discussion group, but occasionally the members conducted memory drills to demonstrate their knowledge. Stonewall Jackson was rumored to have carried only two books with him at all times. One of them was the Bible and the other was a collection of Napoleon's maxims.

4. Henry J. Hunt, "Sworn Testimony before a Joint Committee in Congress, April 4, 1864," *Report of the Joint Committee on the Conduct of the War at the Second Session of the Thirty-eighth Congress* (Washington, D.C.: Government Printing Office, 1865), 452.

5. Comte de Paris, *The Battle of Gettysburg: From the History of the Civil War in America* (1886; reprint, Baltimore: Butternut and Blue, 1987), 129.

6. A. T. Cowell, *Tactics at Gettysburg* (Gettysburg: Gettysburg Compiler, 1910), 36.

7. Ibid., 23.

8. Winfield S. Hancock, "Report to Brigadier General S. Williams, __ __, 1863," OR pt. 1, 368.

9. Glen Tucker, "Hancock at Gettysburg" (paper read at the fourth annual Civil War Study Group program at Gettysburg College, Gettysburg, Pa., August 1, 1961), 7.

10. Winfield S. Hancock, "Letter to Rothermel dated December 31, 1868," Pennsylvania State Archives and Vertical Files at Gettysburg National Military Park (hereafter cited as N.M.P.), folder 5, Participant Accounts, Hancock, 1.

11. John Archer, *"The Hour Was One of Horror": East Cemetery Hill at Gettysburg* (Gettysburg: Thomas, 1997), 11.

12. Jacob Hoke, *The Great Invasion of 1863: General Lee in Pennsylvania* (New York: Thomas Yoseloff, 1959), 299.

13. Oliver O. Howard, "Report of August 31, 1863," OR pt. 1, 702.

14. Cowell, *Tactics at Gettysburg,* 15–16.

15. Byrne and Weaver, *Haskell of Gettysburg,* 103.

16. Edward P. Alexander, *Military Memoirs of a Confederate* (Dayton, Ohio: Morningside House, 1977), 388.

CHAPTER 2

1. James Longstreet, "Lee in Pennsylvania," in *Annals of the War: Philadelphia Weekly Times* (1879; reprint, Dayton, Ohio: Morningside House, 1988), 439.

2. James Longstreet, "Lee's Right Wing at Gettysburg," in *Battles and Leaders of the Civil War: Retreat from Gettysburg, 1884–1887*, ed. Robert U. Johnson and Clarence C. Buel (New York: Castle Books, 1956), 339.

3. Ibid.

4. Ibid., 340.

5. Ibid.

6. Jubal A. Early, "Review of the Whole Discussion," *Southern Historical Society Papers*, 4 (July to December 1877): 257.

7. Ibid., 272.

8. Ibid.

9. James P. Smith, "Paper Read before the Southern Historical Society on April 4, 1905," in *The Gettysburg Papers*, vol. 2, comp. Ken Bandy and Florence Freeland (Dayton, Ohio: Morningside Bookshop, 1978), 392.

10. Early, "Review of the Whole Discussion," 272.

11. Comte de Paris, *The Battle of Gettysburg*, 131.

12. Ibid.

13. Jubal A. Early, "Report of August 22, 1863," OR pt. 2, 470.

14. Richard S. Ewell, "Ewell at Kentz, July 2–3, 1878," Vertical Files at Gettysburg N.M.P., folder 5, Participant Accounts, Ewell, 2.

15. Comte de Paris, *The Battle of Gettysburg*, 131.

16. Samuel R. Johnston, engineer, "Letter to Major General Lafayette McLaws of June 27, 1892," Vertical Files at Gettysburg N.M.P., folder 5, Participant Accounts, Johnston, 2.

17. Ibid.

18. Andie Custer, Licensed Battlefield Guide, Gettysburg N.M.P., conversation with author, January 11, 2003.

19. Johnston, "Letter to McLaws," 2.

20. Samuel R. Johnston, engineer, "Letter to Bishop George Peterkin of December __, 1878," Vertical Files at Gettysburg N.M.P., folder 5, Participant Accounts, Johnston, 2.

21. Ibid.

CHAPTER 3

1. Longstreet, "Lee in Pennsylvania," 425.
2. These figures are based in part on numbers stated in John W. Busey and David G. Martin, *Regimental Strengths and Losses at Gettysburg* (Highstown, N.J.: Longstreet House, 1986).
3. Henry J. Hunt, "The Second Day at Gettysburg," in *Battles and Leaders*, 300.
4. John B. Hood, "Letter from Hood to Longstreet, June 28, 1875," in *The Blue and the Gray: The Story of the Civil War as Told by Participants*, ed. Henry S. Commager (New York: Bobbs-Merrill, 1950), 611.
5. Mark M. Boatner III, *The Civil War Dictionary* (New York: David McKay, 1959), 604.
6. Ibid.
7. George G. Meade, "Report of October 1, 1863," OR pt. 1, 116.
8. Frank C. Gibbs, Battery L, 1st Ohio Light Artillery, "Report of July 4, 1863," OR pt. 1, 662.
9. Charles C. Coffin, *Eyewitness to Gettysburg*, ed. John W. Schildt (Shippensburg, Pa.: Burd Street, 1997), 78.
10. Lee, "Report of July 31, 1863," OR pt. 2, 308.
11. Ibid.
12. Benjamin F. Rittenhouse, "The Battle of Gettysburg as Seen from Little Round Top, Read May 4, 1887," in *The Gettysburg Papers*, vol. 2, comp. Ken Bandy and Florence Freeland (Dayton, Ohio: Morningside Bookshop, 1978), 521.
13. Ibid.

CHAPTER 4

1. Lee, "Report of July 31, 1863," OR pt. 2, 308.
2. Ibid.
3. Lee, "Report of January __," OR pt. 2, 318.
4. Ibid., 320.
5. Hood, "Letter to Longstreet, June 28, 1875," 611.
6. J. B. Robertson, "Report of July 17, 1863," OR pt. 2, 404.
7. Alexander, *Military Memoirs*, 394. The area Hood referred to here was Powers Hill, the site of the Union army's artillery reserve and the ambulances of the II, XI, and XII Corps. Much of the artillery reserve was assigned to the Peach Orchard and elsewhere during this phase of the battle. Hood's scouts were mistaken in believing this supply area was

unguarded. The V Corps, for instance, was in transit there and soon the entire VI Corps would be. Besides, these wagons were fully a mile behind the lines.

8. Hood, "Letter to Longstreet," 609.
9. Ibid., 611.
10. Ibid.
11. J. B. Kershaw, "Report of October 1, 1863," OR pt. 2, 367.
12. Lee, "Report of January __, 1864" OR pt. 2, 318.
13. Hood, "Letter to Longstreet," 609.

CHAPTER 5

1. Antoine Henri de Jomini, *The Art of War*, trans. G. H. Mendell and W. P. Craighill (1804; reprint, Philadelphia: J. B. Lippincott, 1863), 199.
2. Ibid., 197.
3. Ibid., 102.
4. Ibid., 102–3.
5. Lee, "Report of January __, 1864," OR pt. 2, 318–19.
6. Longstreet, "Lee's Right Wing at Gettysburg," 341.
7. Clifford Dowdey, *The Seven Days: The Emergence of Lee* (Lincoln: University of Nebraska Press, 1993), 104–5. At Seven Pines, Longstreet had alleged that he had to wait six hours for Huger, implying he was in position by 8 P.M. To the contrary, Longstreet was crossing Gillies Creek at that time while Huger was kept waiting. Johnston was aware of the falseness of Longstreet's claim with regard to time, but acquiesced toward lending support in his own report. The result was that "Huger . . . was never able to get Johnston's support in holding a court of inquiry to disprove the charges against him."
8. See George A. Bruce, *The Twentieth Regiment of Massachusetts Volunteer Infantry, 1861–1865* (New York: Houghton, Mifflin, 1906), 275. Bruce, who served with the 20th Massachusetts in Virginia, wrote an excellent regimental history but understandably was short in his treatment of Confederate tactical strategy. Like several of his Union contemporaries, he quickly glossed over Ewell's role within Lee's plan. For July 2, he merely noted that "General Lee's plans were for Longstreet to attack the left, and Ewell the right of our lines at the same time." See also George G. Meade, *With Meade at Gettysburg*, ed. George G. Meade, Jr. (1913; reprint, Philadelphia: War Library and Museum of the MOL-

LUS, 1930), 105. Meade also generalized Ewell's role for July 2 and erred when he noted that "at the same time orders were sent to Ewell to cooperate in this attack by a simultaneous advance of his troops against the Federal right." Also see William H. Powell, *The Fifth Army Corps in the Army of the Potomac: A Record of Operations during the Civil War in the United States of America, 1861–65* (New York: G. P. Putnam's Sons, 1896), 545. Powell's description of the specific actions of the Union V Corps is commendable; however, like many Union unit historians writing around 1900, he barely mentioned Lee's plan. Of Ewell's role on July 2, he inaccurately noted that Lee "had given orders to Ewell to attack at the same time with Longstreet." See also John M. Vanderslice, *Gettysburg Then and Now* (Gettysburg: Gettysburg Battlefield Memorial Association, c. 1895), 144. Vanderslice, a sixteen-year member of the G.B.M.A. and a one-time secretary of the "Committee on the Location of and Inscriptions on Monuments," also misrepresented Ewell's role. Even with his great attention to detail on most issues, he inaccurately surmised for July 2 that "[Lee] directed Longstreet to make the attempt, while Ewell should attack Meade's right."

9. Carol Reardon, *Pickett's Charge in History and Memory*, ed. Gary W. Gallagher (Chapel Hill: University of North Carolina Press, 1997), 108, 114–15. On page 114, Reardon notes accurately that after the war, "many Northerners refused to tolerate further what they perceived to be continual blatant expressions of Lost Causism. Even more they disliked monuments to Confederate heroes, they despised the feeling that they were losing the literary war for the history books." In my research, I have detected this same "feeling," from the many Union unit historians, that they wanted the record set straight.

CHAPTER 6

1. Henry J. Hunt, "The Second Day at Gettysburg," 300.
2. Samuel R. Johnston, "Letter to McLaws," 2.
3. Early, "Review of the Whole Discussion," 269.
4. Lee, "Report of July 31, 1863," OR pt. 2, 308; Lee, "Report of January __, 1864," OR pt. 2, 320.
5. Lee, "Report of January __, 1864," OR pt. 2, 320.
6. Meade, "Report of October l, 1863," OR pt. 1, 116.
7. Daniel Sickles, "Absurd in His Tactics," *Philadelphia Weekly Times*, August 16, 1886.

8. Ibid.

9. Coffin, *Eyewitness to Gettysburg*, 78.

10. John W. Stevens, Company K, 5th Texas, "Reminiscences of the Civil War," Vertical Files at Gettysburg N.M.P., folder 7, TX5, 114.

11. William C. Oates, 15th Alabama Infantry, Vertical Files at Gettysburg N.M.P., folder 7, AL15, 2.

12. William C. Oates, "Report of August 8, 1863," OR pt. 2, 392.

13. Longstreet, "Lee in Pennsylvania," 425.

14. J. B. Robertson, "Report of July 17, 1863," OR pt. 2, 404.

15. Henry L. Benning, "Report of August 3, 1863," OR pt. 2, 414.

16. Ibid., 415.

17. Robertson, "Report of July 17, 1863," OR pt. 2, 404.

18. Longstreet, "Lee in Pennsylvania," 425.

19. Robertson, "Report of July 17, 1863," OR pt. 2, 404.

20. J. B. Kershaw, "Kershaw's Brigade at Gettysburg," in *Battles and Leaders*, 333.

21. Kershaw, "Report of October 1, 1863," OR pt. 2, 367.

22. Ibid.

23. Thomas Yoseloff, *Confederate Military History*, vol. 3 (New York: Thomas Yoseloff, 1962), 410.

24. Ibid., 411.

25. Kershaw, "Kershaw's Brigade," 334.

26. Harry T. Hays, "Report of August 3, 1863," OR pt. 2, 480–81.

27. C. B. Brockway, Battery F, 1st Pennsylvania Artillery, Union II Corps, "Letter of March 5, 1864 to David Conaughy, Esq.," Vertical Files at Gettysburg N.M.P., folder 6, PAI-ART-F, 3.

CHAPTER 7

1. Longstreet, "Lee in Pennsylvania," 429. Seemingly contradicting himself in 1895, in his work entitled, *From Manassas to Appomattox: Memoirs of the Civil War in America* (Bloomington: Indiana University Press, 1960), 385, Longstreet stated that he had sent his scouts out during the night of July 2 to find a way "by which we might strike the enemy's left, and push it down towards his centre." This account was closer to what Lee expected, and writing it this way might have been Longstreet's method of smoothing over his earlier claims, which seemingly were insubordinate to Lee's general plan.

2. Longstreet, "Lee's Right Wing," 342.

3. Longstreet, "Lee in Pennsylvania," 429.

4. Ibid.

5. James Longstreet, "Report of July 27, 1863," OR pt. 2, 359.

6. Lee, "Report of July 31, 1863," OR pt. 2, 308.

7. Lee, "Report of January __, 1864," OR pt. 2, 320. Also, the same statement was made in his "Report of July 31, 1863," OR pt. 2, 308.

8. Ewell, "Report of __ __, 1863," OR pt. 2, 445–46.

9. Ibid.

10. Ibid., 446.

11. Smith, "Paper Read before Southern Historical Society," 392.

12. Ewell, "Report of __ __, 1863," OR pt. 2, 446.

13. Alexander, *Military Memoirs*, 388.

CHAPTER 8

1. Lee, "Report of January __, 1864," OR pt. 2, 320.

2. Edward P. Alexander, *Fighting for the Confederacy: The Personal Recollections of General Edward Porter Alexander* (Chapel Hill: University of North Carolina Press, 1989), 244.

3. Lee, "Report of January __, 1864," OR pt. 2, 320.

4. Ibid.

5. Lee, "Report of July 31, 1863," OR pt. 2, 308.

6. Jubal A. Early, "Letter Concerning Causes of Lee's Defeat at Gettysburg, Dated March 12, 1877," *Southern Historical Society Papers*, 4 no. 6, (December 1877): 63.

7. Lee, "Report of January __, 1864," OR pt. 2, 320.

8. Ibid., 321.

9. William N. Pendleton, "Report of September 12, 1863," OR pt. 2, 351.

10. Gettysburg National Military Park has targeted this "dense growth of trees," known as the Codori thicket, for removal as specified in the park's current General Management Plan and is gradually thinning it out.

11. Kathleen R. Georg, "The Objective Point of the Assault: The Clump of Trees or Ziegler's Grove," in *A Common Pride and Fame*, pt. 3, appendix B (in bound form at Library of Gettysburg N.M.P.), 425–65.

12. Ibid., 437.

13. Boatner, *Civil War Dictionary*, 604.

14. Winfield S. Hancock, "Testimony before Congressional Sub-committee in Washington, March 22, 1864," in *Army of the Potomac*, pt. 2 (Millwood, N.Y.: Kraus, 1977), 408.

15. Edward P. Alexander, "The Great Charge and Artillery Fighting at Gettysburg," in *Battles and Leaders*, 361–62.

16. Edward P. Alexander, "Letter to Colonel Gilbert Moxley Sorrel," in *Supplement to the Official Records of the Union and Confederate Armies*, pt. 1, reports, vol. 5, ed. Janet B. Hewett, Noah Andre Trudeau, and Bryce A. Suderow (Wilmington, N.C.: Broadfoot, 1995), 361.

17. Edward P. Alexander, "Alexander, Letter of May 3, 1876 to J. B. Bachelder, Esq.," *The Bachelder Papers: Gettysburg in Their Own Words*, ed. David L. Ladd and Audrey L. Ladd, vol. 1 (Dayton, Ohio: Morningside House, 1994), 484.

18. Edward P. Alexander, "Letter of March 17, 1877, to Reverend J. Wm. Jones, Secretary," *Southern Historical Society Papers* (1877): 102–3.

19. Edward P. Alexander, "The Confederate Assault on Cemetery Hill: How the Whole Attacking Force Melted Away in Blue Musketry Smoke: The Story Graphically Retold," originally *New York Times*, then *Louisville Courier Journal*, July 29, 1881.

20. Ibid.

21. Alexander, "The Great Charge," 361–62.

22. Alexander, *Fighting for the Confederacy*, 255.

23. Ibid., 258.

24. Edward P. Alexander, *Military Memoirs of a Confederate: A Critical Narrative* (1907; reprint, Dayton, Ohio: Morningside Bookshop, 1977), 416–17.

25. See chapter nine for a greater discussion on this issue.

26. Alexander, *Critical Narrative*, 418.

CHAPTER 9

1. Hancock, "Testimony in Washington, March 22, 1864," 408.

2. A. L. Long, *Memoirs of Robert E. Lee: His Military and Personal History* (London: Sampson, Low, Marston, Searle, and Rivington, 1886), 287–88.

3. George E. Pickett, "Letter to Mrs. George E. Pickett dated July 4, 1863," *Confederate Veteran* 21, no. 1 (January 1913): 391.

4. Ibid.

5. Peter Wellington Alexander, *Writing and Fighting the Confederate War: The Letters of Peter Wellington Alexander, Confederate War Correspondent*, ed. William B. Styple (Kearny, N.J.: Belle Grove Publishing, 2002), 165, 173.

6. Longstreet, "Report of July 27, 1863," OR pt. 2, 359.

7. Georg, "The Objective Point of the Assault," 425–65.

8. Ibid., 427–28. (This quote originated from: "John B. Bachelder, February 1, 1894 Report to Colonel C. H. Buehler, GBMA." It is located in the Bachelder Correspondence, New Hampshire Historical Society, microfilm reel 5.) See also Walter Harrison, *Pickett's Men: A Fragment of War History* (New York: D. Van Nostrand, 1870), 183. In 1870, Harrison, inspector general of Pickett's division, wrote, "A small clump of trees made the enemy's centre a prominent point of direction." This single and largely uncorroborated assertion made by Harrison would mutate, through Bachelder, to become the cornerstone for an artificially designed and distinctly landscaped spot called the "high water mark." Interestingly, Harrison did not distinguish the "clump" as belonging to Webb's position. When Harrison visited the battlefield in 1869, Ziegler's Grove was still intact and would have just as easily fit this description. His mention of the "enemy's centre" could also be revealing, considering that that the main Cemetery Hill was the center. Both Lee and Meade accurately referred to Hancock's II Corps line as the left center. Finally, Harrison's choice of the words, "a prominent point of direction" is also significant since Bachelder's trees would not have made that kind of impression in either 1863 or in 1869.

9. Georg, "The Objective Point of the Assault," 428.

10. Ibid., 431–32.

11. Ibid., 430; originated from: Comte de Paris, *History of the Civil War in America*, vol. 3, 650, 654, 663, 665–66.

12. Ibid.

13. Ibid., 434–35; originated from: George T. Fleming, ed., *Life and Letters of Alexander Hays* (Pittsburgh, 1919), 459–60. By 1919, Ziegler's Grove had been replanted and had grown sufficiently.

14. Ibid., 435; originated from: Fleming, *Life and Letters of Alexander Hays*, 459–60.

15. See John T. Dent, 1st Delaware Infantry, "Report of __ __, 1863," OR, pt. 1, 469. Dent was the only participant to make a reference to Pettigrew's or Trimble's men having made a right oblique. He reported:

"These columns overlapped in our immediate front, and made the pressure on our line very heavy, the Pickett column moving on us in an oblique direction from the left, the Pender column moving on us in an oblique direction from the right, both columns converging in our immediate front." Dent stood alone with his right oblique claim. Perhaps what he witnessed was the significant intermingling of Pickett's and Pettigrew's men on his front, as the former attempted to sweep north, and as the latter's left flank was being turned and pressed. Interestingly, the position of the 1st Delaware was and is marked just a few feet from Ziegler's Grove.

16. Birkett D. Fry, "Reply to Chairman Dabney H. Maury," *Southern Historical Society Papers* 7 (January to December 1879): 93.

17. Louis G. Young, "Pettigrew's Brigade at Gettysburg," in *Histories of the Several Regiments and Battalions from North Carolina in the Great War, 1861–65*, ed. Walter Clark, vol. 5 (1901; reprint, Wendell, N.C.: Broadfoot's Bookmark, 1982), 126.

18. Winfield S. Hancock, "Report of __ __, 1863," OR, pt. 1, 374–75.

19. John T. Jones, 26th North Carolina Infantry, "Pettigrew's Brigade at Gettysburg: Written from Culpepper Court House, Virginia on July 30, 1863," in *Histories of the Several Regiments and Battalions from North Carolina* , 134.

20. L. E. Bicknell, 1st Massachusetts Sharpshooters, "Repelling Lee's Last Blow at Gettysburg, IV," in *Battles and Leaders*, 392.

21. Hancock, "Report of __ __, 1863," OR, pt. 1, 374.

22. Georg, "The Objective of the Assault," 435; originated from: Fleming, *Life and Letters of Alexander Hays*, 432.

23. Georg, "The Objective of the Assault," 435–36.

24. *Webster's Ninth New Collegiate Dictionary*, s. v. "salient."

25. Longstreet, "Report of July 27, 1863," OR, pt. 2, 359.

26. Ibid.

27. Fry, "Reply to Chairman," 93.

28. Longstreet, "Report of July 27, 1863," OR, pt. 2, 359.

29. R. E. Rodes, "Official Report, __ __, 1863," OR, pt. 2, 557.

30. Ibid., 556.

31. Ibid., 557.

32. Ibid.

33. Longstreet, "Report of July 27, 1863," OR, pt. 2, 359.

34. Ibid.

35. Ibid.
36. Ibid.
37. Longstreet, "Lee's Right Wing at Gettysburg," 343.
38. J. Walter Coleman (former superintendent of Gettysburg N.M.P.), "Letter of March 17, 1943 to Dr. Douglas S. Freeman," vertical files at Gettysburg N.M.P., folders 2 and 3. Also see Arthur J. L. Freemantle, *Three Months in the Southern States* (1864; reprint, Lincoln: University of Nebraska Press, 1991), 264–65.

CHAPTER 10

1. Fry, "Reply to Chairman," 91.
2. Ibid., 93.
3. Ibid.
4. S. G. Shepard, 7th Tennessee Infantry, "Report of August 10, 1863," OR, pt. 2, 646–47.
5. J. B. Turney, Company K, 1st Tennessee Infantry, "The First Tennessee at Gettysburg," *Confederate Veteran* 8, no. 12 (December 1900): 536.
6. Charles S. Peyton, 19th Virginia Infantry, commanding Garnett's brigade, "Report of July 9, 1863," OR, pt. 2, 385–87.
7. Reardon, *Pickett's Charge in History and Memory*, 8.
8. Birkett D. Fry, "Letter of December 27, 1877, to Colonel John B. Bachelder," in *The Bachelder Papers*, 518–19. Fry's letter to Bachelder did not specify that his brigade "directed" Longstreet's Assault, as did his account written for the *Southern Historical Society Papers* a year and a half later. Instead, in his letter to Bachelder, Fry chose to state that both divisions "dressed" and "aligned" on his brigade. For instance, he stated that he and General Pickett had "an understanding as to the dress in the advance." A few lines down, he repeated that "Garnett . . . having joined us, it was agreed that he would dress on my command." Yet a few more lines down, Fry again wrote that Garnett yelled to him during the charge, "I am dressing on you." The word "dress" or "dressing" was used three times as the preferred expression in this letter to Bachelder. Perhaps under the growing pressures of the North Carolina versus Virginia controversy, and burdened by Maury's appeal to "vindicate the fair name of Pettigrew," Fry's later assertions to the *Southern Historical Society Papers* became bolder.
9. Longstreet, "Report of July 27, 1863," OR, pt. 2, 359.
10. Ibid.

11. Ibid.

12. James Longstreet, "General James Longstreet's Account of the Campaign and Battle," *Southern Historical Society Papers* 5 (January to June 1878): 68.

13. Long, *Memoirs of Robert E. Lee*, 288.

CONCLUSION

1. W. A. Love, "Twin Confederate Disasters," *Confederate Veteran* 33 (August 1925).

2. As mentioned in an earlier note, the Gettysburg National Military Park General Management Plan does call for the removal of the current park Visitor Center and Cyclorama Center, and the restoration of Ziegler's Grove.

3. Abraham Lincoln, "Gettysburg Address of November 19, 1863," 2nd draft, 1st revision (Washington, D.C.: Library of Congress).

4. Judge David Wills, "Letter to Pennsylvania Governor Andrew Curtin of July 24, 1863," Vertical Files at Gettysburg N.M.P., folder 10-1, Development and Care of the National Cemetery.

5. Glenn Tucker, "Some Aspects of North Carolina's Participation in the Gettysburg Campaign," *North Carolina Historical Review* 35, no. 2 (April 1958): 191.

6. Ibid., 192.

7. Henry Kyd Douglas, *I Rode with Stonewall* (Chapel Hill: University of North Carolina Press, 1941), 246.

BIBLIOGRAPHY

PRIMARY SOURCES

Published Documents, Government Documents, and Manuscripts

Alexander, Edward P. "Alexander, Letter of May 3, 1863, to J. B. Bachelder, Esq." *The Bachelder Papers: Gettysburg in Their Own Words.* Edited by David L. Ladd and Audrey L. Ladd. Vol. 1. Dayton, Ohio: Morningside House, 1994.

———. "The Great Charge and Artillery Fighting at Gettysburg." In *Battles and Leaders of the Civil War: Retreat from Gettysburg, 1884–1887.* Edited by Robert U. Johnson and Clarence C. Buel. New York: Castle Books, 1956.

———. *Military Memoirs of a Confederate: A Critical Narrative.* 1907. Reprint, Dayton, Ohio: Morningside House, 1977.

———. *Fighting for the Confederacy: The Personal Recollections of General Edward Porter Alexander.* Chapel Hill: University of North Carolina Press, 1989.

———. "Letter to Colonel Gilbert Moxley Sorrel." In *Supplement to the Official Records of the Union and Confederate Armies.* Pt. 1: Reports. Vol. 5. Edited by Janet B. Hewett, Noah A. Trudeau, and Bryce A. Suderow. Wilmington, N.C.: Broadfoot, 1995.

Alexander, Peter W. *Writing and Fighting the Confederate War: The Letters of Peter Wellington Alexander, Confederate War Correspondent.* Edited by William B. Styple. Kearny, N.J.: Belle Grove, 2002.

Bicknell, L. E. "Repelling Lee's Last Blow at Gettysburg, IV." In *Battles and Leaders of the Civil War: Retreat from Gettysburg, 1884–1887*. Edited by Robert U. Johnson and Clarence C. Buel. New York: Castle Books, 1956.

Brockway, C. B. "Letter of March 5, 1864, to David Conaughy, Esq." Vertical Files at Gettysburg National Military Park. Folder 6, PA1–ART-F.

Byrne, Frank L., and Andrew T. Weaver, eds. *Haskell of Gettysburg: His Life and Civil War Papers*. Madison: State Historical Society of Wisconsin, 1970.

Coffin, Charles C. *Eyewitness to Gettysburg*. Edited by John W. Schildt. Shippensburg, Pa.: Burd Street, 1997.

Coleman, J. Walter. "Letter of March 17, 1943. To Douglas S. Freeman." Vertical Files at Gettysburg National Military Park. Folders 2 and 3.

Douglas, Henry Kyd. *I Rode with Stonewall*. Chapel Hill: University of North Carolina Press, 1941.

Ewell, Richard S. "Ewell at Kentz, July 2–3, 1878." Vertical Files at Gettysburg National Military Park. Folder 5, Participant Accounts.

Fleming, George T., ed. *Life and Letters of Alexander Hays*. Pittsburgh, 1919.

Freemantle, Arthur J. L. *Three Months in the Southern States*. 1864. Reprint, Lincoln: University of Nebraska Press, 1991.

Fry, Birkett D. "Letter of December 27, 1877, to Colonel John B. Bachelder." In *The Bachelder Papers: Gettysburg in Their Own Words*. Edited by David L. Ladd and Audrey L. Ladd. Vol. 1. Dayton, Ohio: Morningside House, 1994.

Hancock, Winfield S. "Testimony before Congressional Sub-committee in Washington, March 22, 1864." *Army of the Potomac*. Pt. 2. Millwood, N.Y.: Kraus, 1977.

————. "Letter to Rothermel dated December 31, 1868." Pennsylvania State Archives and Vertical Files at Gettysburg National Military Park. Folder 5, Participant Accounts.

Harrison, Walter. *Pickett's Men: A Fragment of War History*. New York: D. Van Nostrand, 1870.

Hood, John B. "Letter from Hood to Longstreet, June 28, 1875." In *The Blue and the Gray: The Story of the Civil War as Told by Participants*. Edited by Henry S. Commager. New York: Bobbs-Merrill, 1950.

Hunt, Henry J. "Sworn Testimony before a Joint Committee in Congress, April 4, 1864." *Report of the Joint Committee on the Conduct of the War at the Second Session of the Thirty-eighth Congress.* Washington, D.C.: Government Printing Office, 1865.

———. "The Second Day at Gettysburg." In *Battles and Leaders of the Civil War: Retreat from Gettysburg, 1884–1887.* Edited by Robert U. Johnson and Clarence C. Buel. New York: Castle Books, 1956.

Johnston, Samuel R. "Letter to Bishop George Peterkin of December __, 1878." Vertical Files at Gettysburg National Military Park. Folder V5, Participant Accounts.

———. "Letter to Major General Lafayette McLaws of June 27, 1892." Vertical Files at Gettysburg National Military Park. Folder V5, Participant Accounts.

Jomini, Antoine Henri de. *The Art of War.* Trans. G. H. Mendell and W. P. Craighill. 1804. Reprint, Philadelphia: J. B. Lippincott, 1863.

Kershaw, J. B. "Kershaw's Brigade at Gettysburg." In *Battles and Leaders of the Civil War: Retreat From Gettysburg, 1884–1887.* Edited by Robert U. Johnson and Clarence C. Buel. New York: Castle Books, 1956.

Lincoln, Abraham. "Gettysburg Address of November 19, 1863." 2nd draft, 1st revision. Library of Congress, Washington, D.C.

Long, A. L. *Memoirs of Robert E. Lee: His Military and Personal History.* London: Sampson, Low, Marston, Searle, and Rivington, 1886.

Longstreet, James. "Lee's Right Wing at Gettysburg." In *Battles and Leaders of the Civil War: Retreat from Gettysburg, 1884–1887.* Edited by Robert U. Johnson and Clarence C. Buel. New York: Castle Books, 1956.

———. *From Manassas to Appomattox: Memoirs of the Civil War in America.* Bloomington: Indiana University Press, 1960.

Meade, George G. *With Meade at Gettysburg.* Edited by George G. Meade, Jr. 1913. Reprint, Philadelphia: War Library and Museum of the MOLLUS, 1930.

Norton, Oliver W. *The Attack and Defense of Little Round Top: Gettysburg, July 2, 1863.* 1913. Reprint, Dayton, Ohio: Morningside Bookshop, 1983.

Oates, William C. Vertical Files at Gettysburg National Military Park. Folder 7, AL 15.

Paris, Comte de. *The Battle of Gettysburg: From the History of the Civil War in America.* 1886. Reprint, Baltimore: Butternut and Blue, 1987.

Rittenhouse, Benjamin F. "The Battle of Gettysburg as Seen from Little Round Top, Read May 4, 1887." In *The Gettysburg Papers.* Vol. 2.

Compiled by Ken Bandy and Florence Freeland. Dayton, Ohio: Morningside Bookshop, 1978.

Smith, James P. "Paper Read before the Southern Historical Society on April 4, 1905." In *The Gettysburg Papers*. Vol. 2. Compiled by Ken Bandy and Florence Freeland. Dayton, Ohio: Morningside Bookshop, 1978.

Stevens, John W. "Reminiscences of the Civil War." Vertical Files at Gettysburg National Military Park. Folder 7, TX5.

Vanderslice, John M. *Gettysburg Then and Now*. Gettysburg: Gettysburg Battlefield Memorial Association, c. 1895.

The War of the Rebellion: Official Records. Vol. 27, ser. 1, Gettysburg in 3 pts. Washington, D.C.: Government Printing Office, 1889.

Wills, Judge David. "Letter to Pennsylvania Governor Andrew Curtin of July 24, 1863." Vertical Files at Gettysburg National Military Park. Folder 10-1, Development and Care of the National Cemetery.

Periodicals

Alexander, Edward P. "Letter of March 17, 1877, to Reverend J. Wm. Jones, Secretary." *Southern Historical Society Papers* (1877).

———. "The Confederate Assault on Cemetery Hill: How the Whole Attacking Force Melted Away in Blue Musketry Smoke: The Story Graphically Retold." Originally *New York Times*, then *Louisiana Courier Journal*, July 29, 1881.

Early, Jubal A. "Letter Concerning Causes of Lee's Defeat at Gettysburg, Dated March 12, 1877." *Southern Historical Society Papers* 4, no. 6 (December 1877).

———. "Review of the Whole Discussion." *Southern Historical Society Papers* 4 (July to December 1877).

Fry, Birkett D. "Reply to Chairman Dabney H. Maury." *Southern Historical Society Papers* 7 (January to December 1879).

Longstreet, James. "General James Longstreet's Account of the Campaign and Battle." *Southern Historical Society Papers* 5 (1878).

———. "Lee in Pennsylvania." In *Annals of the War: Philadelphia Weekly Times*. 1879. Reprint, Dayton, Ohio: Morningside House, 1988.

Love, W. A. "Twin Confederate Disasters." *Confederate Veteran* 33 (August 1925).

Pickett, George E. "Letter to Mrs. George E. Pickett dated July 4, 1863." *Confederate Veteran* 21 (January 1913).

Sickles, Daniel. "Absurd in His Tactics." *Philadelphia Weekly Times*, August 16, 1886.

Tucker, Glenn. "Some Aspects of North Carolina's Participation in the Gettysburg Campaign." *North Carolina Historical Review* 35, no. 2 (April 1958).

Turney, J. B. "The First Tennessee at Gettysburg." *Confederate Veteran* 8, no. 12. (December 1900).

Unit Histories

Banes, Charles H. *History of the Philadelphia Brigade*. Philadelphia: J B. Lippincott, 1876.

Bruce, George A. *The Twentieth Regiment of Massachusetts Volunteer Infantry, 1861–1865*. New York: Houghton, Mifflin, 1906.

Bryant, Edwin E. *History of the Third Regiment of Wisconsin Veteran Volunteer Infantry, 1861–1865*. Madison, Wis.: Veterans Association of the Regiment, 1891.

Curtis, O. B. *History of the Twenty-Fourth Michigan of the Iron Brigade, Known as the Detroit and Wayne County Regiment*. 1891. Reprint, Gaithersburg, Md.: Olde Soldier Books, 1988.

Jones, John T. "Pettigrew's Brigade at Gettysburg: Written from Culpepper Court House, Virginia on July 30, 1863." In *Histories of the Several Regiments and Battalions from North Carolina in the Great War, 1861–65*. Edited by Walter Clark. Vol. 5. 1901. Reprint, Wendell, N.C.: Broadfoot's Bookmark, 1982.

Powell, William H. *The Fifth Army Corps in the Army of the Potomac: A Record of Operations during the Civil War in the United States of America, 1861–65*. New York: G. P. Putnam's Sons, 1896.

Sawyer, Franklin. *A Military History of the 8th Regiment Ohio Volunteer Infantry: Its Battles, Marches and Army Movements*. Cleveland: Fairbanks and Company, 1881.

Swinton, William. *Campaigns of the Army of the Potomac: A Critical History of Operations in Virginia, Maryland, and Pennsylvania From the Commencement to the Close of the War, 1861–1865*. New York: Charles B. Richardson, 1866.

Walker, Francis A. *History of the Second Army Corps in the Army of the Potomac*. New York: Charles Scribner's Sons, 1887.

Young, Captain Louis G. "Pettigrew's Brigade at Gettysburg." In *Histories of the Several Regiments and Battalions from North Carolina in the Great War, 1861–65*. Edited by Walter Clark. Vol. 5. 1901. Reprint, Wendell, N.C.: Broadfoot's Bookmark, 1982.

SECONDARY SOURCES
Books, Papers Read at Meetings, Interviews

Archer, John. *"The Hour Was One of Horror": East Cemetery Hill at Gettysburg*. Gettysburg: Thomas Publications, 1997.

Boatner III, Mark M. III. *The Civil War Dictionary*. New York: David McKay, 1959.

Breisach, Ernst. *Historiography: Ancient, Medieval, and Modern*. 2nd ed. Chicago: University of Chicago Press, 1994.

Busey, John W. and David G. Martin. *Regimental Strengths and Losses at Gettysburg*. Highstown, N.J.: Longstreet House, 1986.

Clausewitz, Carl von. *On War*. Edited and Translated by Michael Howard and Peter Paret. Princeton: Princeton University Press, 1976.

Coddington, Edwin B. *The Gettysburg Campaign: A Study in Command*. Dayton, Ohio: Morningside Bookshop, 1979.

Cowell, A. T. *Tactics at Gettysburg*. Gettysburg: Gettysburg Compiler, 1910.

Custer, Andie. Licensed Battlefield Guide, Gettysburg N.M.P. Conversation with author, January 11, 2003.

Desjardin, Tom. Several informal interviews. Summer 1996.

Dowdey, Clifford. *The Seven Days: The Emergence of Lee*. Lincoln: University of Nebraska Press, 1993.

Georg, Kathleen R. "The Objective Point of the Assault: The Clump of Trees or Ziegler's Grove?" In *A Common Pride and Fame*. Pt. 3 Appendix B. (in bound form at Library of Gettysburg National Military Park).

Gramm, Kent. *Gettysburg: A Meditation on War and Values*. Bloomington: Indiana University Press, 1994.

Hassler, Warren W., Jr. *Crisis at the Crossroads: The First Day at Gettysburg*. Tuscaloosa: University of Alabama Press, 1970.

Hoke, Jacob. *The Great Invasion of 1863: General Lee in Pennsylvania*. New York: Thomas Yoseloff, 1959.

Lanza, Conrad H. *Napoleon and Modern War: His Military Maxims*. Rev. ed. Harrisburg, Pa.: Military Service, 1943.

Martin, David G. *Gettysburg: July 1*. Rev. ed. Conshohocken, Pa.: Combined Books, 1996.

Pfanz, Harry W. *Gettysburg: The Second Day*. Chapel Hill: University of North Carolina Press, 1987.

Piston, William Garrett. "Cross Purposes: Longstreet, Lee, and Confederate Attack Plans for July 3 at Gettysburg." In *The Third Day at Gettysburg and Beyond*. Edited by Gary W. Gallagher. Chapel Hill: University of North Carolina Press, 1994.

Reardon, Carol. *Pickett's Charge in History and Memory*. Edited by Gary W. Gallagher. Chapel Hill: University of North Carolina Press, 1997.

Shaara, Michael. *The Killer Angels*. New York: Ballantine Books, 1974.

Stewart, George R. *Pickett's Charge: A Micro-history of the Final Attack at Gettysburg, July 3, 1863*. Cambridge, Mass.: Riverside Press, 1959.

Tucker, Glenn. *High Tide at Gettysburg: The Campaign in Pennsylvania*. 1958. Reprint, Gettysburg: Stan Clark Military Books, 1995.

———. "Hancock at Gettysburg." Paper read at the fourth annual Civil War Study Group program at Gettysburg College, Gettysburg, Pa., August 1, 1961.

———. *Lee and Longstreet at Gettysburg*. Indianapolis: Bobbs-Merrill, 1968.

Wert, Jeffry D. *General James Longstreet: The Confederacy's Most Controversial Soldier: A Biography*. New York: Simon and Schuster, 1996.

Yoseloff, Thomas. *Confederate Military History*. Vol. 3. New York: Thomas Yoseloff, 1962.

INDEX

Page numbers for maps and illustrations appear in bold italic type

145